Rabbit Health in the 21st Century Second Edition

A Guide for Bunny Parents

Kathy Smith

iUniverse, Inc.

New York Lincoln Shanghai

Rabbit Health in the 21st Century
Second Edition
A Guide for Bunny Parents

iUniverse, Inc.

For information address:
iUniverse
2021 Pine Lake Road, Suite 100
Lincoln, NE 68512
www.iuniverse.com

ISBN: 0-595-28137-0

Printed in the United States of America

Contents

Acknowledgements vii

Introduction ix

Being Prepared 1

1. 10 Steps to Better Rabbit Health 2
2. Choosing a Rabbit Veterinarian 7
3. Vet Etiquette 12
4. When to Consult a Veterinarian 15
5. Planning for Emergencies 17
6. What to Have in Your Medical Emergency Kit 21
7. An Ounce of Prevention 23

Common Rabbit Health Issues 31

1. The Importance of Neuters and Spays 32
2. Gastrointestinal (GI) Ailments 34
3. Infections 48
4. Mites and Other Parasites 51
5. Fleas 53
6. Dental Challenges 56
7. Coccidia 64
8. Shedding 65
9. Red Urine 67

Chronic Ailments and Aging Bunnies 69

1. *E. cuniculi* 71
2. Head Tilt 74
3. Bladder Sludge 79
4. Abscesses 85
5. Arthritis/Spondylosis 88
6. Loss of Mobility 91
7. Blindness 93
8. Deafness 96
9. Kidney Disease 99

10.   Liver Disease 102
11.   Heart Disease 104
12.   Cancer 110

Care of the Chronically Ill 118
1.   Are You Willing to Pay the Price? 119
2.   Providing Intensive Care 122

Diagnosis and Conventional Treatments 126
1.   Diagnostics 128
2.   Drugs 142

Alternative Medicine 159
1.   Herbal Treatments 161
2.   Acupuncture and Acupressure 171
3.   Chiropractic 173
4.   Other Alternative Techniques 175

Knowing When to Say Goodbye 178
1.   When Bunny Has Given Up 180
2.   When it is Time, But Bunny is Not Ready 182

Coping with Loss 184
1.   When One of a Pair Dies 186
2.   The Importance of Necropsies 188
3.   Final Arrangements 190
4.   Deciding to Welcome Another Rabbit Into Your Heart 192

Helpful Hints 195

Resources 199

Further Reading 203

ACKNOWLEDGEMENTS

Much of the information in this book is now "second nature" to me. Rabbits have been a part of my family for over 20 years. During many of those years I have participated in a variety of rabbit e-mail groups. Every person who has posted a health-related question or answered such a post has contributed in some way to making this book possible.

When it came time to write the sections on diseases where I had no personal experience, I did research from my personal library of <u>House Rabbit Journals</u>, <u>The Bunny Thymes</u>, <u>The Rabbit Review</u>, and HRS Chapter Newsletters from Chicago, Ohio, San Diego, and Washington (State). I'd like to thank the Editors of these publications and the veterinarians who took time to share their knowledge in an easy-to-understand format. The articles I read during my research are listed, by general topic, in the *Further Reading* section at the end of the book.

I have made a conscious choice **not** to include footnotes in this book. My target audience is the average "bunny parent." As a reader, I personally find footnotes distracting and somewhat intimidating. My goal is to make the information in this book as personal and readable as possible—and footnotes do not fit that strategy.

I'd like to offer special thanks to the following individuals and organizations:

Noella Allan, DVM for her thorough medical review and for her creative title idea.

Barbara Deeb, DVM and Jana Rickel for general wording suggestions and for extensive input and editing on the *GI Ailments*, *E. cuniculi*, and *Loss of Mobility* chapters.

Peter G. Fisher, DVM for reviewing the original <u>Rabbit Health 101</u>, offering corrections and editing suggestions, and for providing a second medical review of the new *GI Ailments* chapter.

Michael J. Murray, DVM for reviewing the first edition of <u>Rabbit Health in the 21st Century</u> and making corrections and suggestions that have contributed to this Second Edition.

Deborah Miles-Hoyt who provided almost all the new information in the *Herbal Treatments* chapter, and Pam Truman, DVM for providing a medical review of this information.

Suzanne Trayhan and Kim Meyer for their help with the *Other Alternative Treatments* chapter.

Vineeta Anand for helping with the information on Cowpile Syndrome.

Carrie Long for cover design for both the first and second editions of <u>Rabbit Health in the 21st Century</u>.

Sari Kanfer, DVM and Zooh Corner Rabbit Rescue for permission to include their drawings in the new *Dental Challenges* section.

All the rabbits who have been part of my family, but especially His Royal Highness King Murray who seems to feel obligated to offer me first-hand experience with a wide variety of medical conditions.

Last, but not least, my husband of 25 years, George, for providing both financial and moral support during this project. When he married me he had no idea of my "rabbit habit." I am thankful to have found a life-partner who has learned to love these precious creatures as much as I do, who never criticizes how much I spend on fresh greens or medical care, and who hurts as deeply as I do when one of our fur-children crosses the Rainbow Bridge.

INTRODUCTION

The idea for this book came to me on the day my precious Smokey lost his five month battle with cancer. I realized how much I had learned about rabbit medicine during those months—and how much more **every** caretaker **needs** to know. I wanted to do something tangible, as a tribute to Smokey's courage. And so I embarked on this project.

If you have not read a book on companion rabbit care, I urge you to do so **before** reading this book. Books such as <u>The Essential Rabbit</u>, <u>Hop to It</u>, and <u>The House Rabbit Handbook</u> focus on the joys of having a rabbit companion. Because of its subject matter, this book necessarily focuses on the more difficult aspects of rabbit care.

I have tried to write <u>Rabbit Health in the 21$^{\underline{st}}$ Century</u> for the average rabbit caretaker—one who has little or no medical background. This book is **not** intended to **ever** take the place of a visit to a veterinarian—if anything, it should increase your contact with your veterinarian. It is intended to give you, as a caretaker, the information you need to play an active and informed role in your rabbit's medical care. Always keep in mind that medicine is not an exact science and different veterinarians have different approaches, all of which may be equally valid. Remember, too, that medicine is a constantly changing field. This book, like all medical writings, will contain some outdated information almost as soon as it is published.

For ease of readability, I have tried to use personal pronouns in a consistent, though perhaps arbitrary, way rather than use the more politically correct he/she construction. I have chosen to use feminine personal pronouns for veterinarians because most of the veterinarians I have worked closely with, and some of the top rabbit specialists in the country, are women. Conversely, I have used masculine personal pronouns when referring to rabbits because my first three rabbits were male.

It took more than two years to complete the original <u>Rabbit Health 101.</u> For the first few months, each time I completed a chapter it seemed I had identified two more to write! While writing the book, I lost my long-time bunny companion Choca Paws, adopted a trio, and fostered several rabbits. Each rabbit has given me a new perspective on some aspect of rabbit medicine. While marketing <u>Rabbit Health 101</u>, I met many wonderful bunny people from around the world. It has been a rewarding experience, despite a few unexpected bumps in the road—some of which necessitated the revisions that led to the first edition of <u>Rabbit Health in the 21st Century</u>.

In this second edition you will find many more references to Murray, who has taken it upon himself to give me first-hand experience with as many medical problems as possible. So it seems appropriate that this second edition of <u>Rabbit Health in the 21st Century</u> features His Royal Highness King Murray on the cover and is dedicated to Him—my gray hare who has given me gray hair!

All profits from my **original** <u>Rabbit Health 101</u> and the first edition of <u>Rabbit Health in the 21st Century</u> went to the rescue groups who sold the book. I plan to continue to share the profits from this and future editions of <u>Rabbit Health in the 21st Century</u> with groups who help rabbits. If you've found this book helpful and would like to make a difference, get involved with a local rescue group, make a donation, volunteer at a shelter, or just spread the word about the joy of rabbits as household companions. Each of us **can** make a difference!

BEING PREPARED

Your rabbit is obviously an important member of your family. Now—while he is healthy—is the time to make sure you are prepared if he becomes ill. Get to know your rabbit well so you will notice subtle changes in his habits. Locate and establish a relationship with a qualified rabbit veterinarian. Stock up your emergency medical kit. Think through and document your emergency plan. Hopefully you will never need any of these things, but if you do, you will be glad you planned ahead!

Dante joined our family as a young bunny. Hopefully, the medical experience we have gained treating the bunnies who came before him will help him enjoy a long, happy, healthy life with us. (Photo by Kathy Smith)

10 Steps to Better Rabbit Health

Spending time with your house rabbit every day is a wonderful experience for you and your rabbit. It also helps you become intimately familiar with your companion's normal behavior and prepares you to identify subtle changes that may indicate a medical problem. While most rabbit caretakers do not have a formal medical background, there are several reasons why it is important for you to learn as much as possible about rabbit veterinary care:

1.   It is impossible for every veterinarian to know everything about every species, and each member of a species is a unique individual. **You** need to be the expert on what is normal for **your** bunny.

2.   In an emergency, you may have to see a veterinarian who has never seen your rabbit before or who has limited experience with rabbits in general. The more you know about your rabbit's medical history and rabbit health care in general, the better prepared you will be to help an emergency veterinarian care for your rabbit.

3.   Some medical conditions always require a trip to the veterinarian. These include suspected bacterial infections (runny nose or eyes), broken bone(s), very high or very low temperature, bleeding, etc. Other conditions **may** not require a trip to your vet if you act immediately. For instance, if you suspect your rabbit is developing GI stasis, you can begin treating with non-prescription items from a drug store. Home treatment can avoid unnecessary stress for your rabbit caused by a car ride and can save you the cost of a vet visit. However, if you fail to see improvement quickly you must be prepared for a trip to the vet for abdominal x-rays and palpation to obtain a proper diagnosis.

This section will give you the basic tools to ensure your rabbit receives the best medical care possible.

1.   Three very important things **you** need to know about rabbit health care are:

    •   **Amoxicillin can be deadly to rabbits.** Never let a veterinarian prescribe this (or any other **oral** penicillin derivative). Some forms of injectable penicillin are appropriate for specific conditions as discussed in later sections.

- **Rabbits should not be fasted for more than one or two hours prior to surgery.** It is unnecessary and potentially dangerous. Rabbits cannot vomit and therefore are in no danger of aspirating stomach contents. Moreover, it is extremely important to keep a rabbit's GI system moving. If instructed to withhold food or water when scheduling a procedure, discuss your concerns with your veterinarian immediately.

- **Rabbits suffering from GI stasis (slowdown of the GI system) should not be treated surgically unless x-rays indicate a complete obstruction (e.g. stomach is distended and filled with fluid or gas) or all other options have been exhausted.** The success rate for this type of surgery is very low, even with the most skilled of surgeons.

2. **Learn all you can about common rabbit ailments and their proper (and improper) treatments.** For a comprehensive list of medical articles see http://www.morfz.com/rabrefs.html. If you have e-mail access, you might want to subscribe to one or more of the bunny "lists." This is a good way to learn from the experience of other concerned bunny parents and form lasting friendships. See the *Resources* section at the end of this book for internet addresses, more information on bunny e-mail lists, and other helpful resources. **Note:** Keep in mind, that most of the people who post to e-mail lists are **not** veterinarians. E-mail lists and the Internet should **never** be used as a substitute for an exam by your veterinarian!

3. **Observe your rabbit closely and know what is normal for him.** Pay attention to normal activity level. Be conscious of normal food and water intake and individual food preferences. Recognize the normal size, shape, and quantity of droppings—the litter-box often contains the first subtle signs of medical trouble.

4. **Buy a rectal thermometer and learn how to use it. Note:** Do not use a glass thermometer. If you've never taken a rabbit's temperature, ask your veterinarian to show you how. Abnormal (i.e. shallow) placement of the thermometer may result in artificially low readings. The normal range is 101°F–103°F **or** 38°C–39.6°C, and temperatures more than 1°F or ½°C outside this range (either higher or lower) indicate a potential problem that needs medical attention. The normal temperature for an individual

rabbit may fall anywhere within this range, and it is a good idea to know more precisely what is the normal temperature for each rabbit in your family. To determine this, take about five readings on different days and at different times of the day. Record this information and compute the average for each individual rabbit.

Also, learn to recognize normal gum color. Pink is normal; deep red may indicate the early stages of shock; gray or white usually occurs in the later stages of shock and is often accompanied by a dangerously low temperature. To check gum color, lift the lip up and observe the gum's coloration above the teeth. Press gently on the gum and observe what this normal color looks like. Do this now—while your rabbit is healthy.

5.   **Invest in an inexpensive stethoscope and otoscope.** Both can be ordered from pet supply catalogs or purchased at medical supply stores and some pharmacies. Ask your veterinarian to show you how to use these tools and ask her to teach you what to look and listen for. Familiarize yourself with the healthy appearance of each rabbit's ears and the normal sound of breathing, heartbeat, and GI noises.

6.   **Locate a good primary vet, backup vet, and emergency vet before you need one.** Get recommendations from a local rescue group, a shelter that handles rabbits, or friends, then conduct interviews. Some things to cover include:

- Make sure the vet understands your rabbit is an important family member and you are seeking the best medical care possible. This may seem obvious, but many people view their rabbits as "livestock."

- Tell the vet that you want to know, understand, and approve everything that will be done to treat your rabbit before it is done. If the vet is uncomfortable with this, find another vet!

- If money is a concern, find out what kind of payment options are available if expensive or long-term treatment becomes necessary. Many veterinarians will work with you—and asking before the need arises will confirm your commitment to your rabbit.

- Discuss your views on euthanasia. Make sure your veterinarian understands and supports your views. This will put her in a better position to help you through times of crisis.

7. **If in doubt, consult your veterinarian.** If your rabbit "is not acting like himself," it is best to have him checked out. Rabbits are very good at hiding the fact that something is wrong with them. The sooner you consult a veterinarian, the better your chances of catching the problem while it is easily treatable. More options may be available with an early diagnosis, and you will have more time to decide the best course of action.

8. **Make sure you know what procedures and medications the vet is going to use on your bunny before they are used. Don't be afraid to ask questions.** Remember, medicine is not an exact science.

The following are some of the questions you might want to ask:

- What medical condition do you think my rabbit has and how did you reach that conclusion? (Note: Some type of diagnostic test, such as radiographs, cytology, culture/sensitivity, or urinalysis should be used whenever possible to confirm an initial diagnosis.)

- What medication/procedure are you planning to use to treat my rabbit?

- What are the risks associated with this medication/procedure? (Note: Beware if the answer is "none." Few medical treatments are risk-free.)

- What other treatments are available? Why do you recommend this one? (Note: Depending on their other clients, a veterinarian may gravitate toward the least expensive rather than the best treatment.)

- How often have you used this treatment for this condition and what is your success rate?

- What (if any) are the risks of **delaying** this treatment? (Note: You may want to delay treatment so you can weigh the risks, do additional research, or get a second opinion.)

Add your own questions and keep the list in your wallet to refer to in times of crisis.

9.   **Whenever possible, stay with your rabbit while any procedure is being performed.** Your presence and the sound of your voice will help keep your rabbit calm. (I usually just pet my bunny and repeat soothingly, "It's OK sweetheart, it's OK."). You will also know immediately if your bunny is in pain—if so, speak up and ask that the procedure be stopped or modified, or ask that your rabbit be sedated before continuing. **Note:** Some veterinarians allow owners to restrain their animals during simple procedures such as drawing blood. Others do not allow this for insurance reasons. It is a good idea to clarify this with your veterinarian in the early stages of your relationship.

10. **Listen to your gut.** Whether you are selecting a veterinarian, deciding if your rabbit needs to be seen, or deciding whether to proceed with a treatment, listen to the voice inside that tells you what to do. Whether it is intuition, a "guardian angel," or your rabbit telling you what he needs, that voice will help you make the best possible decision for your rabbit.

Murray has played a key role in my "Rabbit Health Continuing Education" program. (Photo by Kathy Smith)

Choosing a Rabbit Veterinarian

Good rabbit veterinarians are hard to find. Rabbit medicine requires special training, understanding, and dedication to keeping up with the latest information. Your rabbit is an important member of your family. You'll need to put some time and energy into finding the right person to trust with your rabbit's life. Remember, too, that quality veterinary care is not cheap. You will be working with a specialist and should be prepared to pay for her expertise.

Don't assume that the clinic down the street or the veterinarian who is so wonderful with a friend's dog or cat is a good place to start. The most dangerous veterinarians are those who don't know about rabbits and won't admit it! If there is a local rescue group in your area, or if you know other people with rabbits, ask for referrals. Don't, however, assume that because a doctor is recommended that she is necessarily right for you.

If you can't get a recommendation, start with the Yellow Pages and call the clinics that mention "Exotics" in their advertisements. Ask if they treat rabbits, and if so, approximately how many a year they see. More is usually better, but not always. Ask if you can schedule a time to talk to the primary rabbit doctor and ask some general questions. You may choose to do this by phone or you may ask to meet the doctor in person and tour the clinic.

Either through recommendations or from the Yellow Pages, try to come up with at least three doctors to interview. (This may mean looking some distance from your home.) Have a standard set of questions that you ask each one. The following are some of the questions you might want to ask and some tips on evaluating the answers you get. Of course, you will want to add your own questions!

1. What percent of the rabbits you see are indoor companions? Outdoor pets? Show/stock animals? More rabbits are not necessarily better if a large percent are considered livestock or live alone in a hutch outside. If the best veterinarian you can find sees primarily these types of rabbits (and this is possible in some areas), you will have to do a lot of educating about your rabbit's role in your family and the lengths to which you are willing to go to keep him healthy. Doctors who treat rabbits as "livestock" are more likely to suggest euthanasia for an ill—or even "imperfect"—rabbit.

2. What diagnostic tools and treatments do you normally use for GI slow-downs? What is your success rate? Avoid any doctor who mentions surgery except as a last resort. They will also probably have a low success rate. Look for doctors who use x-rays to determine whether there is an actual obstruction and treat accordingly. Motility drugs such as Reglan® (metoclopramide) and Propulsid® (cisapride) are excellent if there is no obstruction, but can be deadly if there is. A GI slowdown with no obstruction may be a result of stress or it may be secondary to other physical ailments such as bacterial infections or dental problems. A good veterinarian will treat the GI problem **and** try to find the source of the problem. Regardless of the cause of the slowdown, a good veterinarian will suggest supportive measures such as subcutaneous fluids, abdominal massage, and keeping the rabbit warm. If your rabbit is not eating or drinking on his own, she will probably suggest syringe-feeding to get the GI moving again. Ask what she recommends. Good answers include Oxbow's Critical Care, canned pumpkin (100% pumpkin only, not pie filling), a softened pellet mixture, Ensure or Deliver 2.0, baby foods (avoid those containing onion), or some combination of these. She may also suggest oral fluids including fresh pineapple juice, Pedialyte, or Gatorade. Finally, ask her opinion about pain medication for GI problems. Banamine® (flunixin meglumine) is excellent for this type of pain and can literally make the difference between life and death.

3. When treating infections, what diagnostic tools do you use to determine which medication to prescribe? Beware of a veterinarian who simply prescribes Baytril® (enrofloxacin)—or any other drug—without attempting to identify the bacteria. If you get this answer, ask about doing a culture/sensitivity test. Many veterinarians don't suggest this because clients are unwilling to spend the money. This is one way to communicate how important it is to you that your rabbit be given the best possible care! A good veterinarian should be happy to have you bring up the subject.

When an infection is present, most veterinarians will initiate antibiotic therapy while waiting for results of the culture/sensitivity test. The best diagnosticians do cytology (gram staining and then viewing a sample through a microscope) to visually identify yeast, bacteria, or both. If bacteria are present, it is best to follow up with a culture/sensitivity to determine the drug(s) that will be most effective. A doctor who does cytology well has a better chance of prescribing the right drug initially.

4. Under what conditions (if any) would you prescribe Amoxicillin, Clindamicin, or Erythromycin for a rabbit? The answer should be "Never!" or possibly "Only if every other option has been tried and has failed." **Oral peni-cillin (Amoxicillin, Ampicillin, etc.) or erythromycin can kill your rabbit by destroying the good gut flora. Death can occur shortly after administration of the drug or up to three weeks after the drug has been taken. Injectable Penicillin G is a fairly safe antibiotic for rabbits, though normally not a first-choice drug.** (See sections on Infections and Drugs for more detail.)

5. What types of surgery, if any, have you performed on rabbits? What is your success rate? If a rabbit needs to be sedated or anesthetized for a procedure, what anesthetic do you use? If the doctor you are talking to does not do surgery, ask where she would refer you if surgery were necessary. A veterinarian who does not do surgery may not be a bad choice—an excellent surgeon may be more likely to suggest a surgical solution for conditions that can be treated in less invasive ways. However, if you choose a doctor who does not do surgery, be sure to interview the surgeon as well! Success rates should be high (at or near 100% for routine procedures such as neuters and spays). The safest anesthetic for rabbits is isoflurane gas. It is best if the rabbit is masked rather than intubated unless your veterinarian is skilled at intubation. (For people good at intubating, this is a safer route since there is no chance for aspiration and the airway is preserved through virtually all maneuvering).

6. What is your opinion of de-clawing a rabbit? Rabbits do not have retractable claws like cats do. A rabbit's claws are an integral part of the foot's structure. A rabbit who has been de-clawed has actually had the first phalanx of each toe amputated. Be wary of any veterinarian who doesn't know this.

7. How would you handle a critical illness (for example, cancer) where the care of a specialist was required, but the specialist has no experience treating rabbits? Look for a doctor who is comfortable working as part of a treatment team. If you are lucky (as I was), the veterinarian you are talking to will answer with this approach. If not, ask if she would be willing to be the rabbit specialist in a team environment. Some day your rabbit's life may depend on her answer.

If you are interested in including alternative medicine—herbs, acupuncture, chiropractic manipulation, etc.—as part of your rabbit's health care options, it is wise to find out how your veterinarian feels about these techniques in the early stages of your relationship. Some traditional veterinarians are very open to combining holistic and traditional western medicine; some are skeptical, but still willing to trying non-traditional approaches; and some view holistic medicine as complete nonsense. If you are planning to try holistic treatments, especially herbs, it is **extremely** important for you to be comfortable discussing these treatments with your rabbit's primary veterinarian. As herbs are being used more in both human and veterinary medicine, more **interactions** are being discovered between herbs and traditional drugs. It is important for you to feel comfortable telling your veterinarian about **all** treatments your rabbit is receiving and to know that she will consider interactions between herbs and the medications she prescribes.

You will also want to find out about the doctor's after-hours emergency coverage. If doctors in the clinic rotate being "on call"—or if your vet uses an emergency clinic—ask how much these doctors know about rabbit health. Unless they are equally skilled in dealing with rabbits, ask if your doctor is willing to be contacted (by the emergency doctor) for phone consultations in case of an emergency with your rabbit.

If you don't find a veterinarian you are completely comfortable with during your initial search, identify the "best" candidate(s)—**and keep looking**. Continue asking rabbit friends for referrals and check the Yellow Pages each year for new "Exotics" veterinarians. Be patient and persistent—your rabbit is worth it!

Once you find a veterinarian you are happy with, don't put all your eggs in one basket. Continue your search until you also have at least one good backup. Remember, your primary veterinarian is only human. She will need time off for seminars, vacations, and family emergencies. She may become ill, decide to become a full-time parent, move to another city, or simply "burn out." You need a backup plan.

Every bit as important as a doctor's professional knowledge and skills is her openness to outside information. It is essential that she recognize that you are the expert on what is normal behavior for your rabbit and that she respects your instinct that something is wrong. Equally critical is openness to new information from a variety of sources (including the Internet) and a willingness to consult with other veterinarians if a case is unusual or if your rabbit is not responding to standard treatments. Although it is important for you to have confidence in your veterinarian and for her to have self-confidence, blind trust is dangerous. If at any time you are not comfortable with the treatment she is providing, don't hesitate to get a second opinion. Remember, each doctor has her strengths and weaknesses. When you have a sick bunny, choose a doctor based on the person most qualified to treat the

current problem. Remember, your bunny's life depends on the medical choices you make for him.

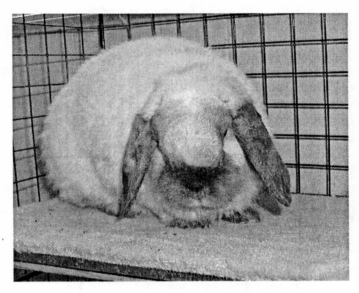

Hemi was lucky to be rescued from the shelter by Kristy. During his neuter the vet discovered his teeth were a mess and many of them had to be extracted. Hemi is thriving on a diet of baby food, softened pellets (imported from Canada) and canned pumpkin. (Photo by Kathy Smith)

Vet Etiquette

A good veterinarian is a priceless asset and should be treated with appreciation and respect. Just as it is important for your veterinarian to understand that you are the expert on what is normal for your rabbit, it is important for you to remember that your veterinarian is a professional with years of training and experience. Although you want her to be open to information from outside sources, she is not likely to appreciate it if you walk in with a copy of an e-mail, an article from the Internet, or this book and try to tell her how to do her job.

Outside information should always be presented as a starting point for discussion with your veterinarian, not a request for specific treatment. If you participate in rabbit e-mail groups, you will find a tremendous wealth of rabbit medical knowledge among the members—both from official rescuers and from individuals who seem to be "magnets" for rabbits with medical problems. However, please keep in mind that most of the people giving medical advice are **not** veterinarians and their knowledge comes from personal experience rather than professional training. Be sure to discuss any medical advice you receive with your veterinarian **before** following it. Remember, your veterinarian is a trained professional who has actually seen your rabbit! She has both general medical knowledge and information about your rabbit's history and condition that might make it inappropriate—or even dangerous—to follow the advice offered on e-mail lists.

When presenting outside ideas to your veterinarian, remember to do so with the appropriate level of respect for her professional expertise. Know how to ask questions and share suggestions in a way that won't make her feel you are questioning her professional judgment. Remember also that medicine is a rapidly changing field and most veterinarians keep up with new developments in the field. What an e-mail group is discussing as a promising "new" treatment may be "old news" to your veterinarian. Before bombarding her with information, ask what **she** knows about the subject and ask if she would be interested in reading the information you have. If there is a specific article you really want her to read, ask if she has time to read it and share her opinions with you during your next office visit—then, be prepared to listen with an open mind even if her reaction is not what you want to hear.

There are times when you will need to ask your veterinarian to consult with another doctor, but this should be the exception rather than the norm. You should usually feel comfortable trying your veterinarian's approach to treating a problem—if not, start looking for a new veterinarian. If your veterinarian is having trouble diagnosing your rabbit's problem, if your rabbit has an unusual condition, or if the normal treatments don't seem to be working, you should be able to ask your veterinarian to consult with a doctor you know has experience with similar problems or with one of the Rabbit Specialists listed in the *Resources* section. If you do ask your veterinarian to consult, offer to pay for her time and the phone call **in addition to** any fee charged by the other doctor. This is only fair since consult calls can be lengthy and normally take place when long-distance charges are high.

It helps to have a good relationship with the entire staff at your Vet Clinic. Here are some tips to help you be the client everyone wants to help:

- Be on time—or even early—for your appointments. If you can't make an appointment—or know you are running late—call to let the office know.
- Schedule appointments as far in advance as possible. It is a good idea to check on all your family members before leaving for work in the morning. If someone seems "off", call your vet early in the day to discuss the situation and see if you should schedule an appointment. Unless you have a true emergency, don't expect to be able to call when you get home from work and have your rabbit seen that day!
- If you have an appointment scheduled and need to take an additional bunny, call first to see if your veterinarian has time or if you need to reschedule. Don't assume she can see two rabbits in the time allotted for one!
- If you need to speak to your veterinarian by phone, you will probably need to leave a message. If your question is not urgent, clearly state that in the message you leave. Your vet will appreciate this help in prioritizing her messages. True, it may take her longer to return your call, but she will probably also have more time for your question. And if your messages are normally "not urgent", an urgent message from **you** will probably result in a quickly returned call.
- Don't expect your veterinarian to diagnose and prescribe treatment over the phone. Unless you are dealing with a recurring problem, your veterinarian will probably need to examine your rabbit.
- If your rabbit is receiving periodic treatment from a technician (e.g. injections or sub-q fluids) and you have questions or concerns, **schedule an appointment** with the veterinarian herself to address these

issues. At the appointment, be organized. Have a written list of the topics you want to cover.

- If you have an emergency and will be at the clinic when they open, leave a message to let them know you are coming in with an emergency. This will help the receptionist know not to schedule anything else new.
- Be patient if you have to wait for an appointment. If your veterinarian is running late, it means she gives **every** animal the time he needs rather than rushing to stay on schedule. Remember also that emergencies happen and you want a veterinarian who will "work you in" if you do have one.

If you have a veterinarian who is wonderful with your rabbit and a staff who cares about you, count your blessings. Take every opportunity to let each person know how much you appreciate them. Always take time to say please and thank you to every staff member who helps you.

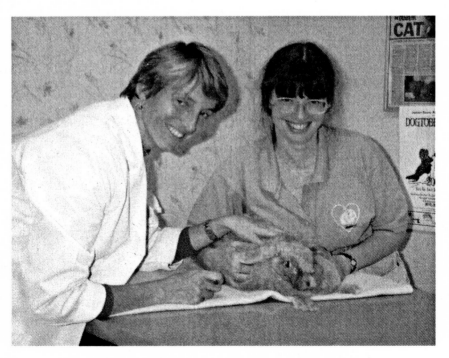

Murray at his weekly checkup with Dr. Allan (left). (Photo courtesy of Lakewood Animal Health Center)

When to Consult a Veterinarian

It would be nice if your rabbit could just **tell** you when something is wrong with him. Instead, most rabbits work very hard to hide the fact that they are ill. As a rabbit caretaker, it is extremely important to know what is normal for **your rabbit**. Daily interaction with your rabbit will help you recognize subtle changes in behavior that may be early symptoms of illness. Symptoms to watch for include:

GI Symptoms
* loss of appetite or changes in eating habits (**Note:** A rabbit who does not eat or drink for 24 hours should be taken to a qualified rabbit veterinarian **immediately**)
* no fecals, small fecals or diarrhea
* sitting in a hunched position or pressing stomach/abdomen to floor
* loud GI sounds **or** complete silence in the stomach (use a stethoscope or listen with your ear pressed against the stomach)

Respiratory and Ear Symptoms
* increased, shallow, and/or labored breathing (watch sides going in and out)
* chest congestion (rattling noises in chest)
* sneezing, nasal discharge, or watery eyes
* scratching or shaking ears

Urinary Tract Symptoms
* straining to urinate
* sitting in the litter-box for long periods of time
* jumping in and out of the litter-box multiple times in succession
* sudden loss of litter-box habits or dribbling of urine
* urine which appears more white, suggesting sludge buildup

General Symptoms
* fever **or** hypothermia (normal temperature is 101°F–103°F **or** 38°C–39.6°C)
* loud teeth grinding (a sign of pain, as opposed to soft tooth "purring")
* irritability or unusual aggressiveness
* listlessness, lethargy, or lack of interest in his surroundings

If your rabbit shows any of these symptoms, make an appointment with a qualified rabbit veterinarian as soon as possible. **Do not wait until it conveniently fits into your schedule.** Seemingly minor symptoms **can** escalate into major emergencies in less than 24 hours—even in the best of homes. If you think you are facing a medical emergency, follow the procedures in the next section (*Planning for Emergencies*).

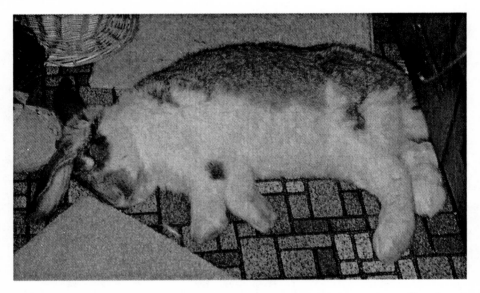

Although this may look like a medical emergency, Thumper is just totally relaxed. This pose is commonly referred to as the "dead bunny flop." (Photo by Kathy Smith)

Planning for Emergencies

The three key elements in surviving a medical emergency with your rabbit are:

1.   Have a well-thought-out emergency plan
2.   Be able to recognize when a medical problem is an emergency
3.   Remain calm while executing your plan

Your Emergency Plan

The first step in your emergency plan is to identify a primary rabbit veterinarian and at least one (preferably two) backup. Have the phone numbers written down and keep them close to the phone. Know the normal schedule (days and hours) of each doctor. Don't trust your memory—write it down next to the phone numbers. If you have several rabbits or one that is critically ill, also try to know their vacation and seminar schedules. This can save precious time in an emergency.

Know the quickest route from your house to each clinic. If your normal route might be clogged during rush hour, try to identify an alternate route as well. Know each doctor's after-hours emergency procedures. If this involves going to an emergency clinic, make a practice trip to make sure you know where it is and the quickest way to get there.

If your doctor's emergency plan involves paging her, calling a service which contacts the doctor, or any other process which involves someone calling you with instructions, **be sure to keep your phone line open after making the call.** Unless you have a separate phone line, this is not the time to "surf the net" for information or e-mail someone for support. Make sure your family stays off the phone until you hear back. If another call comes in, quickly and firmly tell the caller you are expecting an important call and you will have to get back to them.

If you have been trained in first aid and/or CPR, you may want to talk to your vet about showing you how to adapt these procedures—especially CPR and techniques to stop bleeding—for use on a rabbit. Keep in mind that a rabbit's bone structure and internal organs are smaller and more fragile than those of most other animals you would apply these techniques to. Also, be aware that revival techniques such as CPR have a very low success rate in rabbits, even when performed by a skilled veterinarian with the assistance of supportive medications. However, it may give you some comfort to know how to **try** revival techniques, even if they fail.

Identifying an Emergency

If your bunny shows any of the following symptoms, consider it an emergency:

- Shallow breathing and/or weak heartbeat
- Complete immobility or unresponsiveness
- Severe diarrhea (liquid stools) or mucous-covered stools
- Complete silence in the stomach
- Labored breathing
- Convulsions/seizures
- Any injury resulting in open wounds, possible broken bones, or symptoms of shock such as listlessness, limpness, or abnormal gum color (either gray or redder than normal)
- Temperature lower than 100°F (37.7°C) or higher than 104°F (40°C)
- Not eating for 24 hours, no fecals in 24 hours or increasingly smaller fecals
- Dehydration (dry, tacky mucous membranes and/or delayed skin elasticity)
- Grey/white mucous membrane color (e.g. gums)
- Loss of balance or head tilt
- Partial or total paralysis

If you are not sure whether your bunny's condition is an emergency, or if your bunny has been attacked by another animal (even another bunny), assume that you are dealing with an emergency and act accordingly.

Steps to Take If You Suspect a Medical Emergency

If you suspect a medical emergency, stay calm. **Quickly** do the following to assess your rabbit's condition:

1. Take your bunny's temperature if you have not already done so. If the temperature is less than 100°F, try to get the temperature up with a heating pad (on low) or hot water bottle (wrapped in a towel). Prepare a hot water bottle to use on the way to the vet. If your rabbit's temperature is 105°F or higher, moisten his ears and the bottom of his feet with alcohol to help reduce his temperature on the way to the vet.

2.   Check gum color. If gums are redder than normal, your rabbit may be in the early stages of shock. Press a finger against the upper gums. If they don't turn pink after a momentary whiteness, or if the gums are totally white or gray, this can indicate a more serious stage of shock. Get to the veterinarian immediately.

3.   Check for dehydration. Gently lift the skin along the bunny's back. Normally it will snap back into place (although in older bunnies the skin does lose some of its elasticity). If the skin stays up in a ridge, your bunny is severely dehydrated. If you have the setup and know how to administer subcutaneous fluids, administer fluids (warmed unless your rabbit's temperature is above normal) and then go immediately to your veterinarian.

Once you have assessed and stabilized your rabbit's condition, get him to a veterinarian quickly. Based on the day, time, and your veterinarians' schedules, quickly decide where you need to take the bunny. If you are lucky enough to discover the emergency during office hours and you feel you have time, make a quick call to the office to make sure the bunny veterinarian is in the office and let them know you are coming in with an emergency. **Don't** ask for an appointment. Confidently say something like, "This is _____. I have an emergency with my bunny _____. I just want to confirm that Dr. _____ is in before coming in." Don't let them tell you the doctor is "booked." If they try, simply repeat, "This is an emergency—**is she in?**" A word of caution here—most veterinary office visits should be non-emergency. The technique described above may backfire if you have a reputation for **always** waiting until the problem reaches emergency status.

If a family member or neighbor is available immediately, ask them to drive you to the veterinarian's office or emergency clinic. You can then hold your bunny on the trip, monitoring his condition. Talk soothingly to your bunny to help calm him.

If you have never faced an emergency before, expect the following differences between an emergency visit and your normal veterinary appointment:

•   You probably will not be able to stay with your rabbit. He may be taken away for immediate evaluation and/or stabilizing treatment.

•   It may be necessary to leave your rabbit at the hospital, at least until his condition is stabilized, a preliminary diagnosis has been reached, and a treatment started. In other cases, home treatment will be all that is required.

•   Emergency care is difficult for the veterinarian (no matter how skilled she is) and expensive for the client.

•   Despite what some ER shows depict, not all emergency cases are salvageable.

Finally, if you are dealing with an emergency clinic, remember that "emergency" is a relative term. Just as in a hospital ER, patients are not necessarily treated in the order they arrive. If the clinic is busy and your rabbit is taken for immediate treatment, expect a long wait before someone gets back to you with a diagnosis/prognosis.

Goldie is a "miracle bunny" who survived GI surgery after her kidneys shut down and her temperature dropped to 98°F. Dr. Bradley discovered several stomach ulcers and ended up removing a portion of her stomach roughly the size of a quarter. After several days of "round the clock" veterinary care, Goldie came home and recovered completely. (Photo by Kathy Smith)

What to Have in Your Medical Emergency Kit

Wound First Aid

- A wound disinfectant such as betadine, polyhydroxydine solution, or chlorhexidine solution (for cleansing minor wounds, scratches)
- Bag Balm, silvadene cream, or calendula lotion or ointment (for topical application to minor wounds, sores, and scratches)
- Hydrogen peroxide (use diluted)
- Balmax, A & D, or Desitin ointment
- Gauze bandages
- Sterile gauze
- Sterile absorbent bandaging pads
- Butterfly bandage
- Neosporin (**not** Neosporin Plus) or triple antibiotic
- Quik Stop or styptic powder (to stop bleeding of claws **only—do not use on skin. Note:** all-purpose flour will work in an emergency)
- Saline eye wash (to flush foreign matter out of eyes)

Note: Since wounds can lead to abscesses, it is always best to consult your veterinarian before treating a wound.

GI Treatments

- Probiotics (to restore balance of GI flora: Acid-Pak 4-way, Equine Probios, or BeneBac)
- Non-dairy Acidophilus
- Simethicone (to relieve gas symptoms)
- Canned pumpkin for syringe feeding (be sure to get 100% pumpkin, not pie filling with spices)
- A large (5cc or greater) oral syringe for feeding (should have fairly wide tip)
- Coffee grinder for making pellet powder (optional—wash thoroughly if it has been used to grind coffee)
- Lactated Ringer's Solution and fluid administration set (optional—training by a veterinarian is required for use)

Multi-Use

- Pedialyte (to rehydrate and keep hydrated)
- 3cc oral syringes (for Pedialyte or oral medications)
- Pill crusher (optional)
- Pill splitter (optional)
- Ice
- Heating pad or hot water bottle (in case of hypothermia)
- Soft towels
- Eyedropper
- Scissors
- Tweezers
- Cotton swabs
- Sterile cotton balls

Diagnostics

- Infant (rectal) thermometer (should go up to at least 106°F or 41°C)
- KY or other lubricant
- Rubbing alcohol (to clean thermometer)
- Stethoscope (optional)
- Otoscope (optional)

Phoenix, a 10-year-old English Lop, lived a happy life in spite of arthritis, reflux, and a disintegrated joint. She was affectionately referred to as The Flob because the sound she made when she hopped was kaflobba kaflobba. (Photo by Kim Meyer)

An Ounce of Prevention

The adage "an ounce of prevention is worth a pound of cure" holds true for rabbits as well as for humans. The most important things you, as a caretaker, can do to prevent illness or injury are:

- Feed your rabbit a healthy diet
- Provide plenty of exercise time
- Learn to handle your rabbit correctly
- Minimize stress

Healthy Diet

Unlimited Timothy Hay is the most critical element of a healthy bunny diet. It is the best source of fiber, the most important element in keeping your bunny's GI tract moving. Brome, oat, and other grass hays may be provided for variety. Alfalfa hay should be considered a "treat" for **most** rabbits over one year old because it causes weight gain and is higher in calcium. However, for some rabbits—especially the long-haired breeds—timothy hay may not contain enough calories. For geriatric rabbits, overweight rabbits, or rabbits with renal disease, alfalfa hay should be avoided altogether.

When shopping for hay, avoid the packages sold in pet stores. These usually look brown because they are not fresh and therefore do not appeal to your rabbit. If there are rural areas near you, you may be able to buy hay from a farmer (especially one with horses) or a local feed store. Many rabbit caretakers order from the companies listed in the *Resources* section at the end of this book. These companies deliver to your door and have hay available in a variety of quantities. Their hay is fresh, green, and has a wonderful smell.

You can usually request first- or second-cutting hay. If possible, start with a small amount of each to see how your rabbit reacts. First cutting has a higher stem-to-leaf ratio and is coarser. Many people feel first cutting is more fibrous and, therefore, is better for your bunny—if he will eat it. Second cutting is leafier with finer stems and thus has a lower stem to leaf ratio. Many bunnies who turn their nose up at first cutting hay **love** second cutting. Buy what your bunny likes best!

Many caretakers resist providing hay for their rabbit because it is "messy" or because of family allergies. If someone in your home has allergies, put the hay only in your bunny's litter-box or cage and don't have the litter-box/cage in that person's bedroom. Have a household member who is not allergic handle the hay. Unless allergies are severe, this approach should keep allergies manageable. **Remember, there is no substitute for hay!**

One of the most debated topics among rabbit veterinarians, rescuers, and caretakers is the proper balance between hay, commercial rabbit food ("pellets") and fresh produce ("greens"). For years some of the top rabbit veterinarians have promoted a "pelletless" diet (hay and greens only). Pellets were described as foods developed and sold for the convenience of breeders. Many caretakers have reported that their rabbits thrive on this diet and develop diarrhea when fed pellets. Recently, however, a small but growing number of caretakers with rabbits who suffer from chronic or recurrent episodes of "gas" or GI stasis have reported dramatic improvement after switching their rabbits to a diet void of any greens (i.e. just hay and pellets) or a diet where "greens" are fed only as an occasional "treat." An animal nutritionist has suggested that the sheer variety of foods we offer our pampered house rabbits may create GI problems since each food must be digested in a slightly different way, sometimes even requiring a different microbial population. Both commercial rabbit food and fresh produce will be discussed below. If your rabbit has chronic or recurring GI problems, talk to your veterinarian about adjusting the pellets/greens ratio in his diet. If the problem worsens, discuss adjusting the ratio in the **other** direction!

Many experts consider **fresh vegetables** to be an important part of a healthy diet. Suggested amounts vary from one to three cups per day per five pounds of rabbit. If your rabbit does not eat commercial rabbit food, it is important to feed a **variety** of vegetables—**at least** three or four different vegetables from the list below—to ensure proper nutrition. For rabbits who do eat commercial rabbit food, less variety may be better. As always, discuss any proposed diet changes with your veterinarian and observe your rabbit carefully whenever his diet changes.

The following vegetables can be offered to your rabbit:

Greens (mustard, collard, dandelion, etc. **Note:** collard greens are high in calcium and may cause sludge.)
Leaf lettuce (red, green, romaine, escarole, endive, etc. **Note: Feeding iceberg lettuce is strongly discouraged!**)

Herbs (parsley, cilantro, dill, basil, mint, etc.)
Broccoli, kale, cabbage (limit quantities—these are high in oxalates and may cause gas)
Carrots (limit quantities because of natural sugar content) and Carrot Tops (high in calcium)
Radicchio (expensive in some areas)

Fresh fruit may be offered in **small** quantities as a treat—one to two tablespoons per day per five pounds of rabbit. Fruit should be limited because of its natural sugar content. Fruits that can safely be offered include:

Apples
Bananas
Cranberries
Grapes
Pears
Raisins
Strawberries

Always wash fruit and vegetables thoroughly and never feed seeds.

A variety of high-quality commercial rabbit foods are available. Commercial rabbit food is either pelletted (compressed at a relatively low temperature) or extruded (pasteurized at a high temperature). According to a nutritionist at Kaytee Products, extruded food is easier to digest. Pelletted food may be either alfalfa-based or timothy-based. All currently available extruded foods are alfalfa-based.

It is not unusual for rabbits to gain weight after they are neutered. **If your rabbit is becoming overweight,** your veterinarian may recommend limiting commercial food to about 1/8 to 1/4 cup per day per five pounds of rabbit. When buying commercial food, check the label for fiber (at least 16%), protein (not more than 16%), fat (not more than 2-3%), and calcium (not more than 1%). Manna Pro **Double Duty** and Purina **High Fiber** are excellent alfalfa-based pellets, though you may have to work to locate these. Kay-Tee **Rainbow Exact** and Martin Super Premium Rabbit Nutrition (available only in Canada at this time) are extruded foods. Both American Pet Diner and Oxbow offer timothy-based pellets. Either a timothy-based pellet or Kay-Tee Rainbow Exact is recommended for bunnies with bladder sludge, high calcium levels, or renal disease.

Never feed your rabbit the "gourmet" pellets that contain dried fruit, nuts, and/or seeds. These are high in fat and are known to cause health problems. In addition, many contain corn, beans, split peas and/or Canadian Peas (these look like white peas), any of which can be deadly to your rabbit. Also avoid the "treat sticks" sold by pet stores. These contain seeds and often honey, both of which can contribute to GI problems.

The possibility of mycotoxins in commercial rabbit foods (pellets and hay) is another controversial topic in the rabbit community. Mycotoxins are invisible, highly toxic poisons produced when mold (which may not be visible) in the food is shocked by sudden temperature changes. Mycotoxins can be introduced into rabbit food from contaminated raw materials (hay), through the manufacturing process, or by improper storage in the warehouse or in your home. While all reputable manufacturers periodically test food samples for mycotoxins, there is some question as to whether the "acceptable" levels are set too high to be safe for rabbits. In addition, the toxins are often found in "clusters" and are not visible, so the results of sample testing may not always reflect the safety of the entire batch.

While some bunny parents believe that eliminating commercial food from their rabbit's diet is the only way to protect him from the risk of mycotoxin poisoning, there are things you can do to minimize your rabbit's risk:

- Purchase commercial food only from manufacturers with a proven track record. Beware of unknown "bargain brands."

- Whenever possible, purchase pellets in the original, unopened manufacturer's packaging.

- Don't purchase more than the amount of food you will use in a three month period.

- Check the bag's manufacture and/or expiration date. Don't buy a bag that is near its expiration date and throw away any expired food.

- Never buy a bag of food that is damaged, has been wet, or has been stored in a humid environment.

- At home, store pellets in a cool, dry place away from direct sunlight. **Storage containers should not be completely air-tight.**

- Throw away any commercial food that gets wet, shows any visible sign of mold, or simply doesn't look or smell "right" to you.

- If your rabbit suddenly rejects his pellets, consider that there may be something wrong with them. Discard the bag (or return to retailer if it is a new bag) and replace it with another bag with a different expiration date or lot number.

Mycotoxin poisoning can cause a wide variety of medical problems including GI slowdowns and bleeding, a depressed immune system, and sudden failure **or** gradual deterioration of major organs (liver, kidneys, or heart). If several rabbits in your household develop similar vague symptoms at the same time, consider the **possibility** that you may be dealing with mycotoxins.

If you suspect mycotoxin poisoning, contact your veterinarian immediately and ask her to recommend a lab that can test your food. Have blood work done on **all** your rabbits, minimally kidney and liver values. Ask your veterinarian about prescribing an ulcer medication such as sucralfate or Prilosec® to help sooth the GI tract. Finally, change your rabbit's food **immediately**, preferably to a different brand.

The proper balance of hay, vegetables, pellets, and fruit may be different for each rabbit in your home and may change for an individual rabbit as he grows older or as his health changes. Remember, hay is the most important part of your rabbit's diet—if he is not eating **lots** of hay, you may be feeding too many vegetables, pellets, or both. If your rabbit seems overweight, underweight, or if he is gaining or losing weight, consult your veterinarian for recommendations about adjusting his diet. All dietary changes should be made gradually and with your veterinarian's approval.

Exercise

Rabbits should **never** be confined to a cage 24 hours a day. They require a minimum of two to three hours of exercise time per day. The best arrangement is for your bunny to have an entire room or a large run as his primary living space.

If your rabbit is caged much of the time, exercise periods should be offered at roughly the same time each day so a routine can be established. Ideally, exercise time should be during the periods that a rabbit is naturally most active—early to mid-morning and/or late afternoon through late evening. Fortunately, a rabbit's natural schedule fits in nicely with the average working-family's daily routine. There is no better way to start or end your day than by watching your bunny's playful antics.

Of course, it is important to bunny-proof your rabbit's play area. Be sure electric and phone cords are either covered or moved out of bunny's reach. Anything you don't want your bunny to chew on **and all house plants** should also be placed safely out of his reach. Another option is to set up a large "exercise pen" which provides your bunny with a play area and strictly limits his access to cords, furniture, and other things in your house.

Proper Handling

Rabbits are fragile creatures with delicate bone structures. Improper handling can easily cause injury. It is critical that all members of your household learn to handle your rabbit properly and that small children be carefully supervised around him.

The best way to interact with your rabbit is on his "turf"—the floor. Begin by spending time sitting on the floor of your rabbit's area. Read a book, write letters, or talk quietly on the phone. Let your rabbit come up to you for attention. When he does, pet him gently and talk to him soothingly.

There will be times when you need to pick your rabbit up (to trim his nails, take him to the vet, or give medicine). It is wise to get him used to being picked up occasionally by his primary caretaker. However, keep in mind that most rabbits do not like to be picked up and carried. Remember, rabbits are prey animals and being grabbed or lifted off the ground is a frightening experience for them. Instinctively, they may associate these actions with being captured by a predator such as a hawk or owl. When you do need to pick your rabbit up, always take time to explain to him what you need to do and why.

A good way to get your rabbit used to being picked up is to start gradually from your sessions on the floor. Begin by placing a hand under his front arms and slowly lifting his front feet while petting him. Once he is comfortable with this, try lifting him into your lap. To do this, place one hand (usually your right hand if you are right handed) under his front arms, use the other hand to support his hindquarters, and quickly and confidently scoop him toward you. Hold him securely next to your body, petting him and talking soothingly to him. If he begins to struggle, place him carefully back on the ground. If he has let you hold him for a while, consider rewarding him with his favorite treat food.

Once you are able to hold your bunny for a while in a seated position, slowly stand up while holding him firmly. If he begins to struggle, quickly get yourself and the bunny back to ground level and carefully put him down. A rabbit can easily injure himself by struggling in your arms or jumping out of them while you're standing.

Never let anyone pick a rabbit up by his ears or by the scruff of his neck.

Minimizing Stress

We all know that excess stress can kill. This is even more true for rabbits than for humans. Rabbits have delicately balanced digestive and immune systems. Excess stress can bring on an episode of GI stasis or cause a "dormant" disease to become active. The best way to minimize stress for a rabbit is to keep him safely inside your home. Outdoor rabbits, even if they are in a predator-proof hutch or cage, can literally be frightened to death by a **perceived** danger.

Your house rabbit also needs a place he can go for "bunny quiet time." This is especially important if there is a lot of activity in your home or if you have small children. Whether this space is his cage or "his room," it should be in a quiet area of your home. If you do have children, teach them that when your rabbit is in this area, he wants to be alone and they must respect this. Adults, too, should respect a bunny's space. For example, don't invade your bunny's area to clean it when he has retreated there for privacy. Whenever possible, clean his area when he is out playing in another part of the house.

*Herman's mom opened my eyes to the small but growing number of rabbits who cannot tolerate greens in their diet. Six years ago Herman's mom fed him the diet recommended by many rescue groups and some of the top U.S. rabbit veterinarians—unlimited hay, limited pellets, and a wide variety of greens. While many rabbits thrive on this diet, Herman suffered severe bouts of gas and GI stasis several times a year. His veterinarian recommended removing the greens from Herman's diet. Since this was contrary to "conventional wisdom" in the rabbit world, Herman's mom consulted directly with a top rabbit veterinarian who recommended removing **all** pellets from Herman's diet. Herman's GI problems worsened with this diet change and, fortunately, Herman's mom recognized the cause-and-effect relationship. After speaking with a nutritionist, Herman's mom decided to stop feeding greens and return pellets to Herman's diet. Within 24 hours, Herman was feeling better and is a happy, healthy 10-year-old whose diet consists of hay and pellets. Herman's story contains several lessons: 1) There is no one diet that is right for all rabbits. Diet should be tailored to each rabbit's needs. 2) Diagnosis and treatment without a physical exam is risky at best. 3) Consultations should be between veterinarians.* (Photo by Sandy Minshull)

COMMON RABBIT HEALTH ISSUES

This section covers some of the more common rabbit health problems. We have come a long way in the diagnosis and treatment of these problems. In the past, bacterial infections and GI shutdowns were often fatal. Today, a skilled rabbit veterinarian and a watchful caretaker can usually—though, of course, not always—successfully treat the ailments in this section.

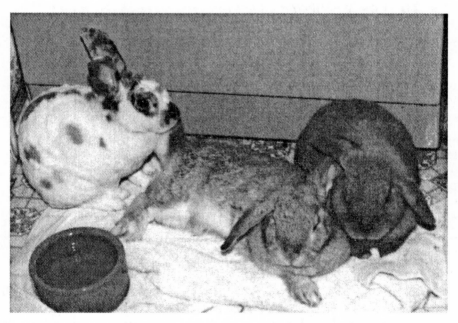

The Three Gifts: Frankie, Goldie, and Murray – named for frankincense, gold, and myrrh. For four and a half years, Murray has had ongoing problems with ear infections and molar spurs. Each episode usually begins with GI stasis. (Photo by Kathy Smith)

The Importance of Neuters and Spays

Rabbits who are neutered or spayed generally make better house pets than rabbits who are intact. Once hormone levels settle down after surgery, litter-box habits usually improve, destructive behaviors such as digging and chewing often stop, and territorial rabbits become more mellow.

Unspayed female rabbits have a very high incidence of ovarian or uterine cancer—as high as 80–90% by age three. Therefore it is important to spay your female rabbit early. If your bunny is older (past the age of four to five years), it is advisable to have a blood chemistry/profile done prior to surgery to ensure the rabbit is in good health. However, don't let your rabbit's age prevent you from having her spayed.

While testicular cancer in rabbits is not widespread, unless your male rabbit is a well-behaved "only rabbit" you will probably want to have him neutered. Intact males are extremely frustrated sexually and often mark territory by spraying urine. Neutering reduces sexual frustration, the need to mark territory, and aggressive behavior. Rabbits are naturally social creatures and most will be happiest with a rabbit companion. An intact male will drive a spayed female crazy trying to mount her—possibly leading to a vicious fight.

Female bunnies can be spayed around the age of four to six months, and male bunnies can be neutered around the age of three to four months (or shortly after the testicles drop). You will want to locate an experienced rabbit veterinarian to perform this procedure. Rabbits are particularly sensitive to anesthesia. The safest anesthesia for rabbits is isoflurane gas, and, unless your veterinarian is very experienced at intubating rabbits, it is best if the rabbit is masked. Some veterinarians use a **low dose** of injectable pre-anesthesia to slightly sedate the rabbit so he is less resistant to the mask.

Pain medication should be given after a neuter or spay. Experienced rabbit veterinarians will often send you home with a dose or two of prescription pain medication (usually, Banamine®, Torbugesic®, Buprenex®, or carprofen)—especially if you request it. If the pain medication you are given is an injection and you have never given a rabbit an injection before, be sure to have your veterinarian show you the proper technique. Pain management can make a big difference in how quickly your rabbit feels like eating after surgery.

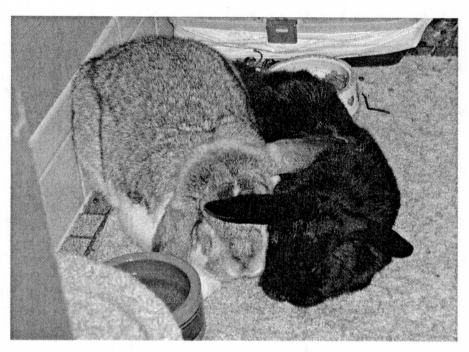

Thumper (left) and Chip are one of those couples that were "meant to be." Chip remained "single" for two years, rejecting all the single males in my household. Obviously she was waiting for "Mr. Right." This picture was taken less than a month after their first meeting at the shelter. (Photo by Kathy Smith)

Gastrointestinal (GI) Ailments

The Rabbit's GI Tract

As a bunny parent, you should have a basic understanding of your rabbit's GI system so you can better understand the GI ailments which may affect your rabbit. The GI system begins at the esophagus and goes through the stomach into the small and large intestines, including the cecum and colon. Rabbits produce two distinct types of "droppings":

- **Fecal pellets** are the hard, round, waste pellets that are normally found in the litter-box (or may be used to mark territory).

- **Cecotropes (cecals)** are soft, dark, shiny, and shaped like a cluster of grapes. Rabbits eat their cecals, usually directly from the anus. While this may seem "gross" to humans, it is a normal and necessary fact of rabbit physiology. Rabbits absorb essential nutrients from their cecals. If your rabbit's GI system is functioning normally, you will probably never see his cecals.

As part of the digestive process, fiber is separated into large and small fiber particles. Large fiber particles form fecal pellets. Smaller fiber particles and excess starches and sugars are sent to the cecum for further digestion. Excess cecal production may indicate a diet too high in starches (bread, oats, etc.) or "sweets" (fruit, carrots, etc.). A balanced diet is critical to maintaining a healthy GI system. Most veterinarians recommend unlimited timothy hay along with a combination of high-quality commercial rabbit food and fresh produce in a ratio that meets your **individual** rabbit's nutritional and digestive needs.

Signs of GI Ailments

If you observe your rabbit carefully when he is healthy, you will notice that he eats almost constantly while awake. A rabbit's GI system needs to be kept continuously moving. Whereas it is not unusual for a cat, dog, or human to stop eating for a day or two, a rabbit who does not eat **anything** in a 12–hour period or who does not eat normally for 24 hours should be taken to a qualified rabbit veterinarian.

Rabbits should also **never** be fasted for a prolonged period before surgery. They cannot vomit and, hence, present no risk of aspirating recently ingested food. Some veterinarians do withhold food for an hour or two just prior to

surgery to ensure that the mouth and throat are clear of food. If you are drop-
ping your rabbit off for surgery, take along some hay and his **favorite** veggies to
tempt him to eat after surgery.

GI problems may be a rabbit's first visible sign of many medical problems
including molar spurs; urinary tract, ear, and respiratory infections; and acute
or chronic failure of major organs such as kidneys or liver. Since your rabbit
can't tell you when he is ill, you need to be acutely aware of what is normal for
your rabbit so you can recognize early signs of GI ailments:

1.   **Subtle changes in eating habits.** Your rabbit may stop eating completely,
        eat less than usual, or eat a different "mix" of foods than normal. Some
        rabbits stop eating pellets or "hard" foods like carrots and broccoli.
        Others may stop eating leafy greens or hay. Often a rabbit who is devel-
        oping GI problems will eat more hay than normal and less of other
        foods. While this is what their system probably needs, if these appetite
        changes last for more than a day or two or if they are accompanied by
        changes in fecals and/or cecals, a visit to his veterinarian is advised.

2.   **Changes in the color, size, consistency, or quantity of fecal and/or
        cecal pellets.** The first sign that your bunny is ill may be found in the
        litter-box. If you are a relatively new bunny parent, you may be sur-
        prised to learn that many people who have groups of rabbits living
        together can actually identify each individual rabbit's fecals! (OK, ded-
        icated bunny people are strange—we **have** to be!) Changes to watch
        for include:

        •   Fecals that are smaller, darker, or dryer than normal
        •   Fecals connected by strands of hair (often referred to as a
                "string of pearls")
        •   Fecals that are unusual in shape (not round); they may be
                larger or smaller than normal
        •   Excess cecals (left on the floor uneaten)
        •   Soft stools or diarrhea-like symptoms (since rabbits rarely have
                soft or liquid fecals, soft stools are **usually** unformed cecals)

GI symptoms may occur suddenly or creep up gradually. Whether you need to
consult a veterinarian immediately or can wait up to 24 hours to see if symptoms improve should depend on your answers to the following questions:

- *What symptoms am I observing?* If your bunny is grinding his teeth loudly (indicating pain), has a distended abdomen, is passing mucous-covered stools or mucous only, or if body temperature is below 100°F (37.7°C) or above 104°F (40.0°C), or there are other signs of shock (including complete listlessness), assume you are dealing with an emergency.

- *What is my veterinarian's availability in the next 24-48 hours?* If it is Friday afternoon or Saturday morning and your veterinarian is working, make an effort to get in to see her or at least speak to her on the phone. This is especially important if the emergency veterinarians in your area are not experienced with rabbits. Rabbits, like human children, seem to get sick on the doctor's day off.

Types of GI Ailments

The most common GI ailments seen in rabbits are:

- Gas
- GI Slowdown (often referred to as stasis)—a decrease in GI motility
- Obstructions (blockages—either partial or complete—of the GI tract; often mistakenly referred to as "hairballs")
- Enteritis or enterotoxemia—a buildup of harmful bacteria and/or their toxins in the GI tract.

Rabbits can also experience nausea, though this can be difficult to diagnose since rabbits don't vomit and can't really tell their caretakers they are nauseated. Some medications, antibiotics in particular, can cause nausea. A less common ailment, Congenital Agangliosis, more commonly known as "Megacolon" or "Cow Pile Syndrome," will be discussed briefly at the end of this chapter.

Diagnosis of GI Ailments

Proper treatment of GI symptoms depends on an accurate diagnosis of the nature of the problem. Any time a GI problem persists for more than 24 hours without improvement, a trip to a rabbit-knowledgeable veterinarian is recommended. When you take a rabbit with GI symptoms to the veterinarian, the exam is likely to include the following:

1.   **Detailed questions about your rabbit's recent activity level, appetite, and litter-box habits.** Be prepared to describe in detail the changes in your rabbit's appetite (quantity, food preferences, etc.) and fecals (smaller than normal, fewer than normal, etc.). Your veterinarian will want to know when you first noticed the changes and whether they have worsened or remained fairly stable. If the rabbit lives in a multi-pet household, information about any changes with other pets are also worth noting.

2.   **Thorough physical exam.** GI symptoms often accompany other medical ailments, so your veterinarian will probably:

- take your rabbit's temperature
- check ears and teeth
- listen to heart, lungs, and GI sounds
- palpate the abdomen

Results of this exam will often identify a primary illness, such as an infection or tooth problem. If your bunny is still eating and producing fecals, and if the GI tract feels and sounds relatively normal, your veterinarian may choose to treat **only** the primary illness and have you closely monitor the GI symptoms. However, if GI symptoms are severe, she will probably want to do additional diagnostics so she can aggressively treat the GI problem as well.

3.   **Abdominal X-rays.** Many of the most effective treatments for GI stasis can cause serious problems if there is an actual blockage, so your veterinarian will probably want to take an x-ray to rule out this possibility. Note that the blockage itself is not always clearly visible on an x-ray. However, a veterinarian skilled at reading rabbit GI x-rays can recognize the presence of a blockage from other clues in an x-ray such as a distended stomach filled with fluid and/or gas. If your veterinarian does not suggest an x-ray, you may want to ask if it would be helpful.

4.   **Blood work.** If the physical exam does not uncover an underlying problem and x-rays do not indicate a blockage, your veterinarian may suggest blood work. The results are used to rule out abnormalities (chronic or acute) of major organs such as the liver or kidneys and can also identify a variety of blood conditions useful in forming the diagnosis.

5.   **Fecal exam.** If your rabbit's symptoms include intermittent soft stools or if mucous is present, your veterinarian may suggest fecal tests to check for the presence of coccidia and/or *clostridia*. Since fecal tests

often give false negatives, your veterinarian may decide to treat for coccidia and/or *clostridia* based on clinical signs alone.

Treatments for Gas

It is not unusual for rabbits to have occasional bouts of painful gas. Simethicone is a good thing to have in your rabbit medicine chest. The infant formula, available at drug or grocery stores, can be safely given to rabbits. If your rabbit is not eating normally and appears to be uncomfortable (hunched up or with stomach pressed to floor)—or if you hear loud gurgling noises— you may want to try a dose or two of simethicone. Talk to your veterinarian in advance about proper doses for each rabbit in your family. Simethicone acts mechanically to break up gas bubbles and is safe to give if you **suspect** your rabbit is suffering from gas. Often, after one or two doses of simethicone, your rabbit will be back to normal.

Gentle abdominal massage can also help relieve the pain of gas. Massage gently with your fingers or try an electric vibrating massager (one with a fairly large, flat surface works best). If you don't have an electric massager, try placing your rabbit on a soft towel on top of a running clothes dryer—the dryer's vibration acts like a giant massager. Car rides have also been known to help relieve gas-induced pain. More than one rabbit owner has reported taking their rabbit to the vet for GI pain, only to discover him feeling much more comfortable by the time they reach their destination. Again, vibration from the ride itself appears to help break up gas bubbles.

If your rabbit's symptoms do not improve after one or two doses of simethicone, he is most likely suffering from a GI ailment requiring consultation with an experienced rabbit veterinarian.

Treatments for GI Slowdowns (Stasis)

A slowdown of the normal contractions of intestinal muscles is often referred to as GI Stasis. GI slowdowns may be a stand-alone problem caused by stress, dehydration, insufficient fiber in the diet, or lack of exercise. More often, however, a GI slowdown is the first noticeable sign of another underlying medical condition.

Since painful gas usually accompanies GI stasis, your veterinarian will probably suggest treatments for gas such as those described above. And, once x-rays have ruled out the presence of an actual obstruction, she may prescribe one or more of the following:

1.   **Keep your bunny warm.** One of the most common causes of death during a bout with GI problems is a low body temperature. Rabbits seem to have a low tolerance for GI pain and their entire system tends to "shutdown." At the first sign of GI problems, take your bunny's temperature. If your bunny is suffering from hypothermia (body temperature less than 100°F or 37.7°C), you will need to carefully monitor him until you are sure he is able to maintain a normal temperature (101°F–103°F **or** 38°C–39.6°C). To raise body temperature, use a heating pad (on low) or hot water bottles (wrapped in towels). If you give sub-q fluids, be sure to warm them first.

2.   **Subcutaneous (sub-q) fluids** are one of the best ways to ensure that the contents of the GI tract remain hydrated. Lactated Ringer's Solution (LRS), injected under the loose skin on the rabbit's back, will often make a bunny feel better even if he is not obviously dehydrated. LRS also helps maintain electrolyte balance, which is vital for proper muscle function, including GI muscles! If you've never given sub-q fluids before, your veterinarian can show you how. Unless your veterinarian has advised you not to, LRS can be safely given when you first begin to notice symptoms of a GI slowdown. Unless your rabbit is running a fever, your veterinarian will probably recommend that you give **warmed** fluids. You may warm fluids by wrapping the bag in a heating pad or running the line through a bowl of very warm water. **Note: Do not** warm fluids in a microwave.

3.   **Pain medication** can literally make the difference between life and death in cases of GI stasis. A rabbit in pain won't feel like eating, which exacerbates the stasis and can lead to a downward spiral. Banamine® is an excellent drug for short-term use (up to a week) and is particularly effective against soft-tissue pain, including intestinal pain. It may also help prevent toxins from forming in the intestines. Torbugesic® and Buprenorphine® (both narcotics) and Rimadyl® (an oral anti-inflammatory) have also been used to treat GI pain.

4.   **GI motility drugs** can help get the GI tract moving again. Both Propulsid® (cisapride) and Reglan® (metaclopramide) have been used extensively in rabbits. Reglan (metaclopramide) is an intestinal motility drug that stimulates contractions in the upper GI and has anti-nausea properties. Propulsid® accelerates stomach emptying while stimulating contractions in the lower esophagus and intestines. Because Reglan and Propulsid work on different portions of the intestinal tract, they have a

synergistic effect when used together and are often used together for more severe cases of GI stasis.

Although Propulsid has been withdrawn from general availability for humans due to potentially serious side-effects in a small number of humans, these heart-related problems have not been documented in rabbits. Many veterinarians prescribe Propulsid® for initial treatment of GI slowdowns because it has few side-effects in rabbits and is **relatively** safe for long-term use. However, if your rabbit requires Propulsid long-term, ask your veterinarian about scheduling regular visits to monitor overall health and watch for early signs of heart disease. My Murray was recently diagnosed with cardiomyopathy and an arrhythmia after taking Propulsid for three years. While there is no evidence that his heart disease was in any way caused by Propulsid® (and Murray very likely would not have survived these three years without its use), you and your veterinarian should consider this possibility when assessing the risks and benefits of long-term Propulsid use. **Note: According to The Physicians Desk Reference, Propulsid should not be given with some antifungal drugs including Nizoral® (ketoconazole), with certain antibiotics including Tylan® and Zithromax®, or with the herb hawthorn.**

5.   **Supportive care** is critical to ensure that your bunny keeps eating and drinking. If your bunny refuses to drink much on his own, your veterinarian may have you **carefully** administer oral fluids. She **may** suggest short-term use of Pedialyte® (available in the infant section of drug and grocery stores) instead of water to help restore electrolyte balance. As always, follow your veterinarian's instructions regarding the type, quantity, and frequency of any oral fluids you give. Avoid any fluids containing sugar (which can encourage overgrowth of harmful bacteria in the cecum).

Another way to get liquids into your bunny is to tempt him by **hand-feeding** fresh, wet, leafy greens such as kale or fragrant herbs such as parsley, cilantro, basil, dill, mint, etc. Tempt him with his favorites and avoid feeding unfamiliar vegetables. Also hand-feed grass hay—avoid alfalfa unless this is what your rabbit is used to eating. Sudden changes in diet can cause a clostridial overgrowth. Sick rabbits often thrive on the extra love and attention that comes with hand-feeding. This is much less stressful to most rabbits than the alternative—syringe feeding.

It is **crucial** to keep your rabbit eating. If your rabbit has eaten **nothing** in 12 hours, he may begin to develop gastric ulcers or liver damage. If you cannot tempt your rabbit to at least "nibble" by hand-feeding him, your veterinarian will probably advise you to **carefully** syringe feed him. (See the *Helpful Hints* section for more on syringe feeding.) She may prescribe Oxbow's Critical Care product or she may have you feed "pellet slurry" (a mixture of ground pellets and water). There are also many recipes for pumpkin/pellet mixtures available at:

http://www.rabbit.org/care/recipies.html
http://www.magpage.com/~laurat/petbunny/diet/syringefeed.html

As always, discuss these with your veterinarian before trying them, since some ingredients can aggravate certain GI ailments.

6.   **Appetite stimulants** may be prescribed if your bunny continues to refuse to eat on his own. B-complex vitamins can be administered orally or by injection and, in addition to stimulating appetite, may help replace nutrients your bunny is missing by not producing/eating cecotropes. Periactin® (cyproheptadine) is an appetite stimulant which is available in tablet or suspension form.

Give your rabbit lots of loving attention, but avoid the (natural) tendency to "hover." If you have to handle your rabbit more than he is used to in order to medicate him, take time to explain what you are doing and why it is necessary. Remain calm and reassuring in his presence. Keep in close touch with your veterinarian by phone, but avoid the stress of unnecessary trips with your rabbit—this means you probably **will** need to learn to give fluids and injections at home (if I can learn, **anybody** can).

Do not separate a sick rabbit from his bonded companion(s) unless they have begun to fight or unless your veterinarian **insists** on isolating the sick rabbit so you can monitor food intake and fecal output. If you do separate bonded groups for either of the above reasons, find a way to house them side-by-side so your sick rabbit will not feel abandoned by his mate(s). Unless they are fighting, provide some time each day when they can actually be together.

Once you begin treatment for GI stasis, you must be both patient and diligent. Don't expect improvement immediately. It may take several days or even longer for your rabbit to begin producing **any** fecal pellets and you should expect those to be small, misshapen, and of a variable consistency. It often takes several weeks for the digestive system to return to normal. Remember that you may not always see steady progress, but as long as you keep your vet informed she will let you know whether or not to continue as instructed or to make a change in treatment.

Treatments for Obstructions

Some veterinarians believe that a GI obstruction in rabbits is almost always the **result** of a GI slowdown rather than its cause. This type of obstruction would normally consist primarily of food held together by hair and mucous and the longer this type of obstruction goes undetected, the more likely it is to become dry and hard, making passage through the GI tract difficult. Obstructions can also be caused by ingested hair mats, carpet fibers, fabric, or other foreign matter that your rabbit's GI tract was not designed to digest. If your rabbit is having GI problems and you know your rabbit has eaten something that may be indigestible, tell your veterinarian immediately what was eaten. This type of obstruction is less likely to respond to the treatments discussed below and immediate surgery **may** be the best course of action. As with stasis, early detection and treatment of an obstruction is the key to saving your rabbit's life.

If your veterinarian's examination, which will probably include x-rays, does indicate the presence of an obstruction, GI motility drugs such as Propulsid® and Reglan® **may** make the problem worse by moving the obstruction into a narrower portion of the GI tract, thus turning a partial blockage into a total one, or by forcing the GI tract to continue contracting against the obstruction. However, depending on the size and location of the obstruction, your veterinarian may recommend using motility drugs in conjunction with aggressive efforts to hydrate and break up the contents of the GI tract.

The most important treatment for an obstruction is to try hydrating the mass, allowing it to soften and pass through the GI tract. Depending on the location and type of obstruction, your veterinarian may recommend any or all of the following:

1.   **Oral fluids.** If your rabbit is not drinking adequately, your veterinarian will probably have you syringe-feed water or Pedialyte (available in the infant section of drug and grocery stores). Oral fluids are particularly important if the obstruction is still in the stomach. If, however, the stomach is already distended and filled with fluid, additional fluids may increase the possibility of the stomach rupturing. In this case

your veterinarian may advise you to **limit** oral fluids. As always, listen carefully and follow her advice.

2.   **Subcutaneous fluids**. Regardless of where the obstruction is located, your veterinarian will probably prescribe subcutaneous fluids—probably Lactated Ringer's Solution (LRS)—to both hydrate the mass and maintain electrolyte balance. For rabbits with kidney disease, some veterinarians will prescribe saline solution instead of LRS.

3.   **Enemas**. If the obstruction is in the lower GI tract, your veterinarian may recommend an enema to help hydrate hardened fecal matter. This procedure needs to be performed by a veterinarian since the risk of colon puncture is a real possibility. In addition, too frequent administration of enemas may upset the rabbit's balance of electrolytes.

Digestive enzymes such as papain (found in papaya), bromelain (found in fresh, but not canned pineapple), or Prozyme (sold as an enzyme supplement for pets) **may** help break up an impacted mass by dissolving the mucous that binds it together. If your veterinarian does not suggest these, ask if she sees any harm in trying them. If fresh fruit is available in your area, try tempting your rabbit with fresh papaya or pineapple. Papain and bromelain are also available in powdered form at most health food stores. These can be kept on hand and should be reconstituted in water or Pedialyte immediately before being given.

Once you have given fluids to hydrate the obstruction and enzymes to help break it up, gentle massage, as described under "Treatments for Gas", may help encourage its movement through the GI tract.

Pain medication is equally important in treating obstructions and stasis. See item #3 under "Treatments for GI Slowdowns (Stasis)" for details.

When an obstruction is present, close monitoring by your veterinarian is **crucial**. She will probably want to repeat x-rays until there is a noticeable improvement in the appearance of the GI tract. It is important that you understand and follow her instructions for follow-up visits. If the stomach becomes distended and is filled primarily with fluid or gas, there is a serious danger that the stomach may rupture. At this point your veterinarian may try to relieve the pressure by passing a tube down the throat and into the stomach to siphon off some of the air or fluid. Prozyme or other digestive enzymes can also be delivered directly into the stomach via such a tube. Surgery should be considered only as a last resort.

Survival rates for GI surgery are extremely low—even with the most skilled rabbit surgeon. Even if a rabbit survives the surgery itself, it is very difficult to get a rabbit's GI tract moving again after this type of surgery and many rabbits experience complications such as peritonitis. However, if you have a rabbit who needs GI surgery, **don't give up**—bunnies can and do survive this surgery. In August 1999 my beloved Goldie had a distended, fluid-filled stomach only 24 hours after appearing perfectly normal. After another 24 hours of aggressive treatment for both stasis and obstructions, a second x-ray showed the stomach even more distended. She had emergency GI surgery and was given only a 50/50 chance even though she survived the surgery. In her case, Dr. Bradley found no actual obstruction; however, Goldie had gastric ulcers that were about ready to perforate (which would have killed her instantly). Dr. Bradley removed a portion of her stomach about the size of a quarter. She took Goldie home and provided round-the-clock care for the next four days. Goldie recovered completely, only to succumb to *E. cuniculi* just 11 months later.

Treatments for Enteritis/Enterotoxemia

Enteritis is an inflammation of the intestinal lining. Enterotoxemia is the buildup of harmful bacteria (often Clostridia) in the cecum. These bacteria can produce painful gas and/or deadly toxins. The liver's job is to remove such toxins and, if overgrowth of Clostridia (or other harmful bacteria) is not controlled quickly, the liver may be damaged beyond repair. Passing mucous-coated feces or mucous alone is a key symptom of both enteritis and enterotoxemia. A bunny suffering from either of these conditions will probably need one of the following medication(s) **in addition to** the treatments for GI stasis discussed above.

Questran® (cholestramine) may be prescribed if overgrowth of Clostridia is confirmed or even suspected. Questran binds to the toxins produced by Clostridia, allowing them to be eliminated in the feces. Dosing instructions for Questran should include mixing it with a **generous** amount of water. Be sure to follow these instructions carefully since Questran can dehydrate the intestines if given with too little water. Questran is not absorbed by the body and is very safe if used as directed.

Flagyl® (metronidazole) is an antibiotic that is sometimes prescribed to treat clostridia infections as well as giardia and other GI infections. Sulfasalazine, a combination sulfa antibiotic and non-steroidal anti-inflammatory, has also been successfully used to treat enteritis by controlling pain and reducing inflammation of the intestinal lining along with its antibacterial effect.

Other Treatments Your Veterinarian May Recommend for GI Ailments

1.   Lactobacillus powder (available at health food stores) or probiotics such as Benebac® or Probios® (available at feed stores or from your veterinarian) **may** help your rabbit by helping restore the proper balance of bacteria in the GI tract. These treatments probably won't hurt and are most likely to help if your rabbit has been taking antibiotics. **Do not** give yogurt to a rabbit who is already experiencing GI upset—use lactobacillus powder instead. While some rabbits like yogurt and handle it well, your rabbit's GI system was never intended to process dairy products.

2.   Some veterinarians prescribe petroleum-based laxatives (Laxatone® or Petromalt®) hoping they will lubricate an obstruction and help it pass through the GI tract. However, these products may actually do more harm than good. They can produce a Vaseline®-like coating which prevents fluids from reaching the mass and softening it. Sometimes veterinarians recommend regular use of Laxatone or Petromalt as a preventative measure; however, regular use of these products can interfere with the absorption of some vitamins and so should never be given before meals.

3.   Your veterinarian may prescribe antibiotics if your rabbit is suffering from GI stasis and if:

   •   Enteritis or enterotoxemia is suspected

   •   Bacterial infection (which may have caused the GI symptoms) has been diagnosed or if your rabbit's immune system may be compromised

   Remember, however, that many antibiotics have the potential to create GI problems. If you are not sure why an antibiotic is being prescribed, discuss your concerns with your veterinarian.

4.   **Some** veterinarians believe that feeding cecals from a healthy rabbit will help re-establish the balance of bacteria in the cecum. However, it may be stressful to the donor rabbit to "harvest" cecals and will probably be stressful to the recipient to be forced to accept them. Discuss these concerns with your veterinarian if instructed to do this.

Mega-colon or "Cowpile Syndrome"

Congenital Agangliosis, also known as "Mega-colon" or "Cow Pile Syndrome," is a hereditary disorder of the gastrointestinal tract found in some rabbits with the "English Spot" or En En color gene. These rabbits are generally white with dark black or brown rings around their eyes and black or brown spots on their back. The symptoms of the disorder include big, misshapen, soft fecals, frequently covered with mucous, and a drippy bottom alternating with long, painful bouts of GI slowdown or stasis. The disorder is believed to be caused by a misdevelopment or malfunction of the colon and/or cecum. During the spells of stasis, it is possible to feel large masses of fecal material with the consistency of ropes of play dough when the rabbit's belly is palpated. Before arriving at this diagnosis, fecal tests are recommended to eliminate the possibility of parasites or a bacterial imbalance or overgrowth in the GI tract.

Rabbits with this disorder have trouble extracting essential nutrients from food, may not produce cecals, and frequently have difficulty maintaining weight. Some rabbits experience recurrent attacks of severe GI stasis. This condition is nearly always "episodic" in nature, characterized by flare-ups followed by periods of relative improvement.

Epsom salts have proven helpful in managing some of the unique symptoms of this disorder. Epsom salts pull fluids into the GI tract which can help soften food matter in the GI tract and also decrease the leakage of mucous and fluid that causes the wet bottom. Epsom salts should be used in conjunction with both dietary supplements and standard stasis treatments (motility drugs, subcutaneous and oral fluids, pain medications, etc.) as deemed appropriate by your veterinarian. When giving Epsom salts, be sure to keep your rabbit adequately hydrated.

A watchful, diligent caretaker and an understanding, resourceful veterinarian are the keys to managing this condition long-term while retaining quality of life. Exercise, adequate hydration, and proper diet (as defined by you and your veterinarian based on your rabbit's individual needs) are especially critical for a rabbit with this condition. Equally important is a caretaker's ability to recognize the early signs of a "flare-up" and follow a well-defined treatment plan as soon as symptoms appear.

Long-Term Implications

Unfortunately, many rabbits who have experienced GI ailments seem to have periodic recurrences of the problem. The good news is that, as a caring rabbit parent, you will become better at recognizing the problem at an early stage and may learn things you can do at home (e.g. diet adjustments, treating hypothermia, and/or giving sub-q fluids) to stop an attack before it requires veterinary care. A proper diet is especially important for a rabbit with recurrent GI problems. Always provide unlimited timothy hay—even if you are convinced your rabbit never eats it! Some rabbits do best with a very small amount of pellets or no pellets at all; others do best with high-quality pellets alone or with a very limited amount of greens. Work closely with your veterinarian to determine the mix of pellets and greens that works best for **your rabbit.**

Veterinarians across the country seem to be seeing more house rabbits with GI ailments. One reason for this may be that more bunny parents are aware of what to watch for and are seeking veterinary care. Another possibility is that house rabbits are more likely to be "spoiled" with treats high in carbohydrates and sugars—and such treats contribute to GI problems. We all know how hard it is to resist a rabbit who is begging for his favorite treat. Next time your rabbit begs for just a little more bread, banana, or cookie, ask yourself this question, "Do I love him enough to say NO?"

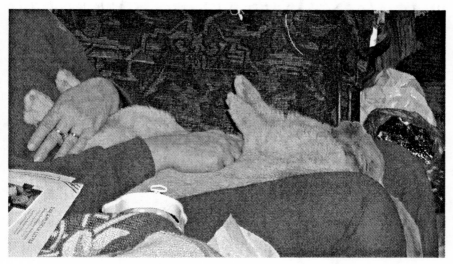

Stormy thoroughly enjoyed the tummy massages he received when he suffered from severe gas. **Note:** *Not all rabbits will be this cooperative!* (Photo by Sue Bergstrand)

Infections

Bacterial and Yeast Infections

Most infections in rabbits are caused by bacteria or yeast and require aggressive medical treatment. The most common infections include:

- **Upper Respiratory Infections** Symptoms often include sneezing (with or without a discharge), runny eyes, and/or chest congestion. Do not assume your bunny has a cold and the infection will go away by itself.

- **Ear Infections** Symptoms may include head shaking, scratching of the ears, and/or a sensitivity at the base of the ear. Runny eyes can also be the first sign of an ear infection. Ear infections that are not caught early can lead to head-tilt—an inner ear condition that causes dizziness and loss of balance. Lops seem to be more susceptible to ear infections, perhaps because the lop ears create a warm, moist environment that encourages growth of bacteria and yeast.

- **Urinary Tract Infections** Symptoms may include sudden loss of litterbox habits, dribbling of urine, straining to urinate, or a "wet bottom." Sometimes a veterinarian will suspect a urinary tract infection based on your rabbit's reaction to having his abdomen gently palpated.

Diagnosis and Treatments of Bacterial and Yeast Infections

Both respiratory and ear infections can be caused by either bacteria or yeast. Antibiotic therapy is actually one of the causes of yeast overgrowth, so it is important to know whether the pathogen is a bacteria or yeast.

Cytology allows a good veterinarian to quickly determine whether bacteria, yeast, or both are present. It involves taking a sample from the infected area and examining the stained sample under a microscope. In cases of a bacterial infection, especially chronic or resistant cases, a culture/sensitivity test will help to further identify the bacteria and the most appropriate antibiotic. However, use of cytology improves the chances that the drug therapy prescribed initially will help (or at least not hurt) your rabbit while waiting for the culture/sensitivity results.

If your veterinarian suspects a bacterial infection, she will probably want to do a deep nasal, eye, or ear culture or a urinalysis to identify the pathogen causing the infection and the drugs to which it is sensitive. If she doesn't suggest doing a **culture/sensitivity test**, ask if it would be helpful. Often, veterinarians will hesitate to suggest such diagnostic tests because many of their clients are not willing to pay for it. To ensure accurate results, the test should be done before the rabbit is started on antibiotics.

If cytology suggests a bacterial infection, most veterinarians will go ahead and start a course of antibiotics while awaiting the results of the culture/sensitivity. This is fine. If the test shows a different rabbit-safe antibiotic would be more effective, your veterinarian will probably switch antibiotics. Don't be surprised if she wants to continue the antibiotic at least two weeks **after the symptoms are gone** to ensure that the bacteria is completely eliminated.

For some types of infections—especially ears, eyes, and wounds—your veterinarian may prescribe either topical or systemic medications or a combination. For severe respiratory infections, your veterinarian may suggest nebulizer treatments in addition to systemic antibiotics to deliver medication more directly to the respiratory system.

For severe or persistent infections, the same antibiotic may be prescribed in both systemic and topical forms. Alternatively, two systemic antibiotics from two different drug classes may be prescribed concurrently, giving a synergistic effect. Usually this consists of a drug that can safely be used long term (for example, a fluoroquinolone such as Baytril®, Ciprofloxacin, or Dicural®) and one that should only be used short-term (for example, an aminoglycoside or injectable penicillin).

Beware of any veterinarian who diagnoses *Pasteurella* (often referred to as "snuffles")—or any other specific bacterial infection—without doing a culture/sensitivity test. While *Pasteurella* is a common cause of upper respiratory disease in rabbits (particularly rhinitis), it is not the only cause. *Pseudomonas aeruginosa, Bordatella bronchiseptica, Streptococcus,* and *Staphylococcus* infections are all frequently mistaken for *Pasteurella* because the symptoms are very similar.

On rare occasions, a rabbit may have a fever but no respiratory discharge or area that can be cultured and no symptoms of a urinary tract infection. In this case your vet will often prescribe a broad-spectrum antibiotic even though she is unable to do additional tests to confirm the diagnosis.

Warning: Never accept a prescription for amoxicillin or any other ORAL form of penicillin for your rabbit.

Viral Infections

Although most infections in rabbits are caused by bacteria rather than a virus, there are two exceptions worth noting:

- **Myxomatosis** is a virus transmitted by biting insects such as fleas or mosquitoes. Symptoms include swelling in or around the face; red, puffy eyelids, lips and/or genitals; and lesions especially on the face or eyelids in addition to lethargy, fever, decreased appetite, and increased water consumption. Luckily, myxomatosis is relatively rare in the U.S. In most other countries a vaccine is available. While **most** rabbits die from myxomatosis, a few do survive. If you suspect myxomatosis, see your veterinarian immediately. Treatment with antibiotics, NSAIDS (to control inflammation and pain), a warm environment, and intensive nursing care can improve your rabbit's chance for survival. More information on myxomatosis is available online at www.kindplanet.org/myxo.html (article written for caretakers) and www.kindplanet.org/myxo2.html (article written for veterinarians).

- **Rabbit Viral Hemorrhagic Disease, or VHD** (also known as RHD, RCV, or RCD) is a highly contagious disease caused by a calcivirus which affects only domestic rabbits and the **European** wild rabbits from which they are descended. It can be spread via **any** object that has come in contact with an infected rabbit. It frequently causes sudden death with no prior symptoms of illness. Bleeding from the nose, mouth, or rectum is sometimes seen. Fortunately, VHD is extremely rare in the U.S., since no vaccine is available here in the U.S. as there is in most other countries. There is no treatment or cure for VHD. The USDA requires "extermination" of all rabbits that may have come in contact with an infected rabbit as well as prompt notification of any suspected cases in the hopes of containing further spread of the disease. More information on VHD is available online at www.kindplanet.org/vhd.

Mites and Other Parasites

Fur mites are particularly difficult to see on rabbits. Symptoms of fur mites may include:

- loss or thinning of hair along the shoulders and middle back of the rabbit
- dandruff-like flakiness
- itching

If you have very sensitive skin, **you** may also experience some skin irritation after coming into contact with a rabbit with fur mites.

Skin scrapings can be obtained and the mites can sometimes be seen under a microscope, but not always. If fur mites (Cheyletiella) are suspected, the best treatment is Ivermectin® once every 10 to 14 days for three to four treatments. For really severe cases, a kitten dose of Advantage® (also used to kill fleas) may be applied in addition to the Ivermectin. Advantage should **not** be used in rabbits who are very young (less than six months), geriatric, or whose general health is compromised.

Ivermectin is also effective against **roundworms, lice,** and **ear mites.** If ear mites are present, it is wise to check for a secondary bacterial ear infection which may require antibiotic treatment.

Other parasites and the recommended treatments include:

- Tapeworms—Droncit®
- Pinworms—Panacur® (fenbendazole)

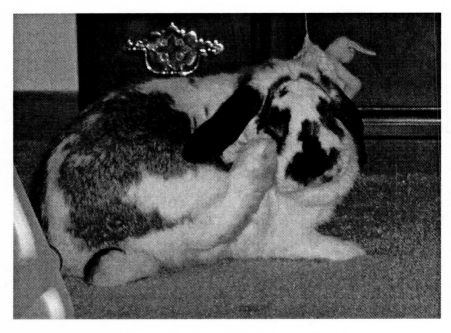

Fred gave me quite a scare one morning when he acted like he was having a seizure. A thorough exam by Dr. Bradley revealed that he simply had a severe case of furmites! (Photo by Sue Bergstrand)

Fleas

If your rabbit seems to have only a few fleas, the safest way to get rid of them is to use a flea comb. A thorough combing should be done daily. Kill the fleas by dipping the comb in warm, soapy water. Rinse the comb thoroughly before continuing to comb.

If you have other animals in your home, first try treating **them** with topical or oral products and use the flea comb approach for your rabbit. Usually, once you have eliminated the fleas on your other animals, your rabbit's problem will go away as well.

If the flea problem is more severe, you can dust your rabbit with 5% carbaryl insecticide (a common brand name is 5% Sevin Dust). Using your hands, gently work the dust down through the fur to the skin. As always, consult your veterinarian **before** using this product and advise her immediately of any changes in your rabbit's behavior after application. **Do not allow your rabbit to be given a flea bath or flea dip.**

Several prescription flea control products have become available for dogs and cats in the last few years. **It is important to realize that none of these products have been formally tested or approved for use in rabbits.** However, most have been tried on rabbits with the following results:

- Advantage®—Many top rabbit veterinarians have reported success using a kitten dose of Advantage (imidacloprid). There have been some deaths reported, although the deaths have not been directly attributed to Advantage. Advantage should not be used for very young (less than six months), elderly (six years or older), or compromised rabbits. It is also wise to remember that your rabbit may have an asymptomatic and thus undiagnosed condition that could make Advantage a dangerous choice.

- Program®—Program (lufenuron) is being used by many top rabbit veterinarians in the country. Program is an oral chitin inhibitor. (Chitin is the material that makes up the exo-[outer]skeleton of the flea. Mammals do not make chitin or have an exo-skeleton and therefore are not affected by lufenuron). Program keeps new eggs from hatching. It does not affect adult fleas, so animals with severe infestation may also require treatment with the insecticidal products discussed above.

- Revolution®—Revolution (selemectin) is now being routinely used by some rescue groups (and their veterinarians) on rabbits who come to them from shelters. Revolution kills adult fleas and prevents eggs from hatching. It is also effective against several types of mites and ticks. Like Advantage and Program, it should be used with caution, especially on rabbits who are older or may have other health problems.

Never use the following products on a rabbit:

- Frontline®—The country's top rabbit specialists strongly advise that Frontline (fipronil) **is not safe for rabbits.** Several rabbits have died or experienced seizures after receiving treatment with Frontline. Although the active ingredient is not supposed to cross into the central nervous system of mammals, the number of rabbit deaths reported suggests this is not true for rabbits.

- Sentinal®—Some veterinarians have switched from Program to Sentinal for dogs. Sentinal has the same active ingredient as Program, along with a heart-worm preventative for dogs and should not be used on rabbits.

As always, let your trusted veterinarian help guide you to the best treatment choice for your rabbit. She should have access to the latest information on safety and effectiveness of the latest prescription treatments for fleas.

If you have had more than a minor flea problem, you may need to treat your rabbit's environment as well. You can treat carpets annually with sodium polyborate (boric acid) or fenoxycarb (an insect growth regulator in the form of a synthetic hormone). The boric acid product made by Flea Busters is safe for both rabbit and owner and has been reported to be very effective by many rabbit parents. You can also try salting your carpet with common table salt. The salt acts as a desiccant when it comes in contact with flea eggs or larvae—the same effect that salt has on slugs or snails. Salt should be reapplied after vacuuming.

For linoleum and other washable surfaces, clean with Murphy's Oil Soap, a natural, vegetable-based soap with a pleasant fragrance that also acts as a flea repellent. Wash bedding, small rugs, and other washable fabrics in hot, soapy water.

Harrison arrived in foster care with a severe case of fleas. (Photo by Kristi Cole)

Dental Challenges

Dental problems are not unusual in rabbits and they are certainly the most common problem in my household. Molar spurs and other dental problems are among the more common underlying causes of GI stasis, so it is important to recognize symptoms as early as possible. As with most ailments, early identification and treatment of minor dental problems is the key to preventing more serious problems.

Your Rabbit's Teeth

A basic understanding of your rabbit's dental structure is the first step in understanding the variety of dental problems that rabbits can have. Rabbits shed their fetal teeth around the time they are born and develop their 28 permanent teeth during the first five weeks after birth. These teeth are made up of:

- Six incisors (front teeth): two large upper and two large lower incisors, plus two much smaller "peg" teeth that are often completely hidden behind the larger upper incisors
- Ten premolars: six upper and four lower
- Twelve molars: six upper and six lower

Premolars and molars are indistinguishable from each other. You may hear them referred to collectively as "cheek" teeth or simply as "molars." A rabbit's lower jaw (mandible) is narrower than the maxilla (upper jaw) and when the jaws are closed, the lower cheek teeth lie inside the upper ones. There is a noticeable gap, called the diastema, between the incisors and the premolars. This gap may be large enough for you to slip your little finger between without feeling teeth (not something I recommend trying with **most** rabbits).

We're all familiar with a rabbit's characteristic incisors, but many rabbit caretakers are not consciously aware that rabbits have cheek teeth until they have a rabbit with dental problems. Incisors and cheek teeth serve two distinct functions: Incisors are used to grip, nip, and slice food; cheek teeth are used to crush and grind food using a relatively horizontal motion when compared with human chewing.

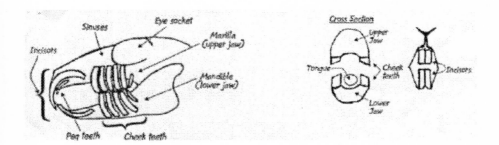

Figure 1: Normal Rabbit Teeth (courtesy Sari Kanfer, DVM and Zooh Corner Rabbit Rescue)

Wild rabbits (including the European rabbit from which our pet rabbits have descended) "graze" almost continuously in order to absorb sufficient nutrients from grass and other plants. Rabbit teeth have evolved to withstand this constant wear. A rabbit's teeth grow continuously throughout his life; however, not all teeth grow at the same rate. Incisors grow faster than cheek teeth and lower cheek teeth grow faster than upper ones. Diet affects the rate of both growth and wear on the teeth. Diets that are high in roughage and coarse fibrous vegetation may help keep teeth worn down which may help **prevent** dental problems from occurring. Dr. Sari Kanfer (who graciously allowed me to use the drawings from her article *Dental Problems in Rabbits*) now recommends a wide **variety** of grass hays and fresh grasses (instead of timothy hay **only**) because the different textures require different chewing mechanics, which in turn help teeth wear more evenly. She also recommends offering safe twigs (available from Zooh Corner Rabbit Rescue and other bunny-friendly suppliers listed in the *Resources* section) as another way to keep cheek teeth worn down.

Types of Dental Problems

Malocclusion (teeth misalignment) is the most common dental problem in rabbits. Malocclusion can occur in the incisors, cheek teeth, or both. If all of your rabbit's teeth come together properly, the act of chewing will probably keep your rabbit's teeth at the proper length despite their continuous growth. However, few rabbits have perfect teeth, and because the upper and lower jaws have different numbers of teeth, a problem with a single tooth in one jaw can affect up to 3 teeth from the opposing jaw.

The most noticeable form of malocclusion is when the incisors don't come together properly. Top or bottom teeth may stick out of the mouth. If they grow inward and remain unnoticed, bottom teeth may poke into the roof of the mouth. Top teeth may actually curl around, forming a circle, and grow back into the gums. Rabbits with this type of malocclusion almost always have difficulty eating hard foods such as carrots and broccoli unless they are cut into small bites.

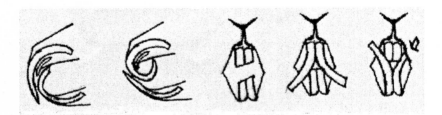

Figure 2: Maloccluded Incisors (courtesy Sari Kanfer, DVM and Zooh Corner Rabbit Rescue)

Molar spurs are another fairly common dental problem. Since molars grow more slowly than incisors, molar problems may show up in older rabbits who have not previously had problems with their teeth. Spurs can occur if cheek teeth are maloccuded, if your rabbit's diet has insufficient roughage to keep the teeth sufficiently worn down, or if his lateral chewing pattern is disturbed for other reasons, such as tooth or ear pain. Spurs on lower teeth most often point toward the tongue, eventually causing either bruising or laceration. Spurs on upper teeth more often point outward, lacerating or bruising the inside of the cheek. However, it is **possible** for points or spurs to be found on **either** side of both upper and lower cheek teeth.

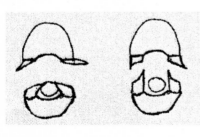

Figure 3: Molar Spurs (courtesy Sari Kanfer, DVM and Zooh Corner Rabbit Rescue)

Maloccluded teeth that continue to grow **can** eventually lead to more serious dental problems. Maloccluded teeth will sometimes develop elongated roots which can penetrate deeper into the jawbones, sometimes causing a tooth root or bone abscess. Elongated tooth roots in the upper jaw can also press on the adjacent tear duct, thus contributing to eye discharge problems.

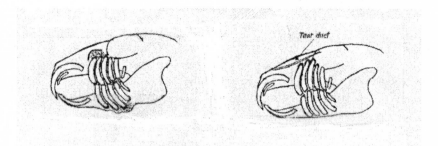

Figure 4: Elongated tooth roots (courtesy Sari Kanfer, DVM and Zooh Corner Rabbit Rescue)

Causes of Dental Problems

As mentioned earlier, diet can play an important role in preventing dental problems. Diet is especially important during prenatal development and during the first five weeks of life when permanent teeth are developing and emerging for the first time. However, it is never too late to work on improving your rabbit's diet! Pellets alone do not require sufficient crushing/grinding to keep cheek teeth worn evenly. Hay plays an important role in keeping your rabbit's teeth healthy. If your rabbit's GI system tolerates leafy greens (without causing recurrent episodes of gas or stasis), these can also help keep teeth worn down.

While diet plays a major role in many dental problems, genetics are also an important factor. Some rabbits are born with obvious dental problems such as an overbite or underbite. Others have teeth that appear normal at birth but seem to have a genetic predisposition for problems later in life. Dental problems are more common in certain breeds of rabbits—specifically the Netherland Dwarf and many lops, especially those with "flat" faces. Pure breed rabbits seem to have more dental problems than mixed breeds, perhaps because of inbreeding. Some veterinarians who neuter and spay rabbits for shelters and rescue groups routinely check teeth while they have the rabbit under anesthesia. If you adopt from such a group, ask whether a dental exam was done and make a note of any problems found during the exam.

Temporomandibular joint problems (TMJ) can also sometimes result in malocclusion. Chiropractic adjustments can often be helpful in relieving the discomfort of TMJ, though residual dental problems may persist. Physical trauma that results in broken or injured teeth can also lead to malocclusion.

Diagnosis

With the exception of incisor malocclusion, which is often quite noticeable, the early signs of most dental problems are subtle enough that even a perceptive caretaker may fail to notice that anything is wrong. Each rabbit has a different tolerance for discomfort. Some rabbits, like Murray and Stormy, will stop eating when molar spurs are minor. Others may continue to eat until there is a severe laceration on the cheek or tongue. To help catch dental problems early, pay attention to normal eating habits and food preferences for each of your rabbits and periodically feel along the outside of the jaw line with your fingers to detect any swelling or sensitive areas. Schedule a dental exam immediately for your rabbit if you notice any of the following:

- Sudden avoidance of "hard" foods such as carrots and broccoli
- **Any** noticeable shift in preferred foods
- Decreased appetite
- Weight loss
- Wetness and/or hair loss on underside of chin (often a symptom of excessive salivation)
- Accumulation of food on the underside of the chin or front paws
- Unpleasant odor to the breath
- Noticeable lump either on the outer cheek below the eye or on the underside of the lower jaw

Remember, however, that some rabbits can have dental problems with minimal or even no clinical signs!

Your rabbit's dental exam will probably begin with your veterinarian checking your rabbit's cheek teeth using an otoscope and visually inspecting his incisors. Depending on the results of this initial exam as well as your rabbit's medical and dental history, clinical signs, and any risk factors (such as age, breed, or siblings with dental problems), your veterinarian may want to anesthetize your rabbit since it is impossible to do a **complete** exam of a rabbit's mouth and teeth without anesthesia. Even under anesthesia, points are not always visible.

Stormy had razor-sharp spurs once that Dr. Allan could detect only when she ran her finger between the teeth and cheek!

While your rabbit is under anesthesia, your veterinarian will normally check general anatomy/alignment and examine carefully for loose or discolored teeth and areas of infection. She may suggest skull x-rays to further identify molars that need to be watched carefully and to check for elongated tooth roots and/or tooth root abscesses. These x-rays are nearly always done while your rabbit is under anesthesia since it is important for his head to be kept still.

Treatments

Maloccluded incisors need to be ground down or trimmed periodically, as often as every two to three weeks or as infrequently as every six months. Most rabbits do not need to be sedated for this procedure. Although I personally recommend having a veterinarian trim incisors, some caretakers I know have had their veterinarian show them how to do this at home, are comfortable doing it, and feel it is less stressful for their rabbit. Sometimes the teeth will improve gradually with regular trimming, allowing trimmings to be needed less frequently. Smokey's incisors originally required trimming every three to four weeks. His teeth gradually improved and within a couple of years we were trimming them only two or three times a year.

If your rabbit's incisors require trimming frequently and show no signs of improving, or if veterinarian visits are very stressful to your rabbit, you may want to talk to your veterinarian about removing the incisors surgically. Incisor extraction is a relatively major procedure since the roots of a rabbit's incisors are quite deep, and occasionally, even with a very skilled surgeon, the incisors will grow back. However, most rabbits who have had their incisors removed do quite well, and for many their quality of life improves without the problematic teeth. Lauren came to us with no upper incisors and lower ones that grew out of her mouth toward her nose. Her incisors required trimming every three to four weeks, and because of the complete absence of opposing teeth, there was no possibility this would ever improve. She has been much happier since having them removed. She is able to eat hay and pellets with no trouble and does well with diced carrots and greens torn into small pieces.

Your veterinarian will treat molar spurs by trimming the spurs and/or filing the teeth until the surface is flat and smooth. If cheek teeth are unusually long or of uneven lengths, your veterinarian will probably try to file them to a uniform length to encourage them to wear more evenly. Veterinarians who do a lot of rabbit teeth often use special dental tools, including a device to hold the mouth open, freeing both hands for working on the teeth.

Molar filing is almost always done while your rabbit is under anesthesia. Many veterinarians use isoflurane (or other gas anesthesia) for this procedure while a few prefer injectable anesthesia. The advantage to isoflurane is that your rabbit wakes up more quickly and will probably have fewer side-effects from the anesthesia. There are a few veterinarians who do molar filing using a mouth gag and **no** anesthesia. You should consider this option **only** if your veterinarian is **completely** comfortable with the procedure **and** you both agree that your rabbit's temperament is suitable for such a procedure. For most rabbits, the risk of using anesthesia is less than the risk of stress caused by being awake during this procedure!

Treatment for tooth or tooth root infections/abscesses usually involves systemic antibiotic therapy and, as with all infections, I recommend doing a culture/sensitivity to ensure that the antibiotic chosen will be effective against the infection. Depending on the severity and extent of the infection, your veterinarian may need to flush the area and/or surgically remove the abscess or infected tooth. She may also pack the area with antibiotic beads to provide continuing antibiotic therapy. **Note:** Cheek teeth should **not** be extracted unless they are loose, infected, or have abscessed roots. Molars must be extracted very carefully, even if they are loose, to avoid breaking the rabbit's jaw.

With the exception of simple incisor trimming, most of the dental procedures, including molar filings, have the potential to cause some lingering pain or discomfort. Some rabbits begin eating immediately after having their molars filed while others may take up to a week before they are eating normally. If your rabbit seems to have a low threshold for discomfort or is slow to resume eating, ask your veterinarian about prescribing pain medication and/or Reglan®, which both stimulates GI motility and helps alleviate nausea.

Long Term Implications

Many rabbits with dental problems have ongoing problems and require close monitoring by their caretaker and veterinarian. If your rabbit has molar spurs, your veterinarian will probably recommend scheduling periodic checkups to catch problems **before** they affect your rabbit clinically. The frequency of rechecks will be different for each rabbit and may change for an individual rabbit over time. Some rabbits need their molars filed as often as every other week for a while—this was true for Murray at one point, although now we are able to go five to ten weeks between filings. Other rabbits may never require molar filing more than once or twice a year. And if you are lucky you may have a rabbit like my Dante who had a single episode of spurs two years ago and has not yet had a recurrence.

If your rabbit has dental problems of any sort, it is a good idea to discuss diet with your veterinarian. Most rabbits adapt quite well to dental problems once their caretakers find the right diet for them. Hay is an important part of your rabbit's diet, but some rabbits with either incisor or molar malocclusion have great difficulty eating hay. Many times I have watched Murray pick up a strand of hay, try for several minutes to eat it, and become completely frustrated! If pellets are the easiest food for your rabbit to eat, discuss the options with your veterinarian. A few people who have rabbits with chronic molar problems have reported slight improvement (increased time between filings) when they began feeding Kaytee Rainbow Exact. It is **possible** that either the larger pieces or the fact that this is an extruded (vs. pelleted) food may help increase tooth wear. Rabbits with more severe molar problems (including loss of many teeth) may only be able to eat soft foods. Many rabbits, including my friend Kristy's Hemi, do quite well on a diet of baby food, canned pumpkin, and softened pellets!

Rabbits with dental problems can make **wonderful** house pets. They are often (though not always) **unable** to chew through phone and electrical cords, rip up carpet, or gnaw woodwork and furniture. You may save more than enough in "home repair" costs to pay for those extra veterinarian visits!

Coccidia

Coccidia are parasites that are commonly found in rabbits but only occasionally cause disease. Many rabbits are "carriers" and their immune system keeps the parasite under control. When they are stressed or their immune system is compromised, an overgrowth of the parasite may cause symptoms that include diarrhea and/or inability to maintain weight.

The presence of this parasite can often (but not always) be detected by having your rabbit veterinarian perform a fecal exam (sometimes called a fecal float). If coccidia are present in the fecals of a symptomatic rabbit, your veterinarian will most likely prescribe a 10-day treatment with Albon® suspension. After the treatment, your veterinarian may want to repeat a fecal exam to confirm that the parasite has been eliminated.

Most species of coccidia are confined to the intestinal tract and only cause serious problems if severe diarrhea is left undiagnosed and untreated. However, there is one species that attacks the liver, and this form of coccidia can be fatal, especially in young rabbits.

Coccidia are highly contagious. If a symptomatic rabbit shares a litter-box or play area with other rabbits, your veterinarian may want to treat all the rabbits in the group or at least do a fecal float on all.

Stormy had a severe case of coccidia when he was rescued. After a 10–day treatment with Albon, he became a happy, healthy cuddle-bun. (Photo by Kathy Smith)

Shedding

Rabbits shed four times a year, alternating between heavy and light sheds. If you have multiple rabbits, they may or may not shed at the same time. Some rabbits seem to shed almost overnight while others may take several weeks to complete a shed.

Each rabbit has a unique shedding pattern which may change over the years. Some rabbits seem to shed equally across the entire body. Others will seem to shed on one part of the body at a time, often developing small bald spots. Often shedding begins at the head with the shedding pattern slowly moving toward their tails.

When your rabbit is going through a heavy shed, it is important to help by brushing or gently plucking the loose hair with your hands. If your rabbit won't tolerate brushing or plucking, try moistening your hands before petting your rabbit (the loose hair will stick to your hand) or pet him with a lint roller.

You may want to offer **fresh** pineapple to your rabbits when they are going through a heavy shed since fresh pineapple contains an enzyme that may help break up masses of food/hair in the GI tract. Canned pineapple does not have the same effect because the canning process destroys the enzyme.

When one rabbit in a group is going through a heavy shed, keep a close eye on the appetite, activity level, and fecals of all members of the group. Remember that rabbits are fastidious groomers and that grooming each other is a sign of affection and acceptance. During heavy shedding periods, find time each day to brush, pluck, or pet away loose hair to minimize the amount of hair that can be ingested. Rabbits cannot vomit, so it is important to watch for any sign of a GI slowdown and begin treatment immediately, especially when your rabbit or his companions are experiencing a heavy shed.

Long-haired rabbits or their mates **can** get "hairballs" from licking and ingesting too much hair. The best way to prevent hair buildup in the stomach is to keep the GI tract moving—and the best way to keep the GI moving is to feed unlimited amounts of timothy and other grass hays and to encourage your rabbit to get plenty of exercise.

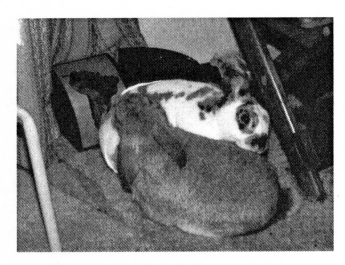

*Frankie and Goldie are pictured here in a mutual grooming session. This common practice makes it important to carefully watch the behavior of **all** rabbits in a group any time **one** of them is going through a heavy shed.* (Photo by Kathy Smith)

Red Urine

Red urine—in the absence of clinical symptoms of urinary tract problems—is not normally a cause for concern. A rabbit's normal urine color can range anywhere from clear to pale yellow to dark yellow, brown, orange, and even bright red. Urine color can change for a variety of reasons including dietary changes, medications, and weather changes. Often the color of a rabbit's urine changes for reasons his caretaker cannot identify. As long as your rabbit is not an unspayed female and is acting normal otherwise, it probably is unnecessary to consult a veterinarian. Urine color will probably return to what you consider normal within a few days.

Red urine in an unspayed female is often caused by a bloody discharge associated with uterine cancer. Rabbits do not have menstrual periods. If you notice red urine in an unspayed female, consult your veterinarian immediately. If the urine is red because of blood, an emergency spay will probably be necessary. If no blood is found in the urine, count your blessings and schedule her spay immediately!

The first time most caretakers see red urine, they assume there is blood in the urine and worry about a urinary tract infection (UTI). However, blood in the urine is often not visible to the naked eye. Watching your rabbit's behavior in the litter-box is a much better way to detect a UTI. Is he straining to urinate? If so, you will notice your rabbit sitting in the litter-box for an unusually long time with his tail very high in the air. If your rabbit is straining to urinate, have him checked by his regular veterinarian as soon as possible. A UTI or bladder sludge may be the cause. If he is straining and **no** urine is produced, there may be a blockage; play it safe and consider this an emergency.

Physical trauma—such as a fall or a blow to the body—can also cause blood in the urine. This diagnosis should be made only after urinalysis and blood work have ruled out the possibility of infection **and** if trauma seems possible based on the rabbit's recent history or normal behaviors (e.g., jumping from high places on a regular basis).

Chip is a healthy spayed female whose urine is often red. (Photo by Kathy Smith)

CHRONIC AILMENTS AND AGING BUNNIES

The conditions discussed in this chapter can strike your rabbit at any age, though some—such as arthritis, blindness, deafness, failure of the major organs (liver, heart, and kidneys), and cancer—seem to be more common in older bunnies. The common thread between all the conditions in this chapter is that they require **long-term** treatment and supportive care.

For some of the conditions in this section veterinarians now have quite a bit of experience and can recommend treatments and supportive measures that have been used successfully on many rabbits. The keys to successful treatment of these conditions include:

- Early recognition that your rabbit has a problem. The earlier these problems are caught, the better the chance of full recovery.

- Finding a veterinarian who can correctly diagnose the **source** of the problem and who keeps up on the latest therapies. Treatment of symptoms—though important in making your rabbit more comfortable—is not enough. It is important to find the underlying cause and attack it aggressively.

- Continuing to treat the condition (if recommended by your veterinarian) even after symptoms have disappeared.

- Watching carefully for any signs of recurrence.

For other conditions, like cancer, many veterinarians may have experience treating these ailments in dogs and cats, but few have experience with them in rabbits. Here we are truly breaking new ground—and these are the areas where it is most important for us to share what has been tried, what has worked, and, equally important, what has failed in rabbits. When the prognosis is grim but the bunny is a true fighter, you may decide to venture into uncharted territory in the hopes of prolonging life (with quality) **and** contributing to the knowledge base that will help other bunnies down the road. The skilled and trusted veterinarian that you worked so hard to find is **essential** on this journey.

Finally, you may wonder whether the long-term care required is worth the effort. Treatment of an ill rabbit can be exhausting and discouraging, but it is worth the effort. The bond you develop with a rabbit during a long-term illness is incredibly deep.

Li'l Bit is a 16-year-old rabbit who has survived the last four years because of the watchful care and resourcefulness of his mom. Both a cart and herbs have played a key role in his survival, allowing Li'l Bit to live a relatively normal and very happy life. (Photo by Deborah Miles-Hoyt)

E. cuniculi

Encephalitozoon cuniculi (*E. cuniculi*) is a protozoan parasite. It forms spores that are shed in the urine and can remain viable in the environment for 30 days or more. Bunnies may contract it at a young age, possibly from an infected mother, or later in life from an infected companion, or by playing in contaminated dirt.

Once the parasite is ingested it gets inside a monocyte (a kind of white blood cell) and travels through the body. It seems to primarily attack the liver, kidneys, and brain. Common symptoms include head tilt, liver failure, kidney failure, loss of function in the legs (back, front, or both), nystagmus (eye twitching), and/or other neurological symptoms. It can also cause blindness by initiating the formation of cataracts.

Diagnosis

E. cuniculi is currently diagnosed by a blood test (ELISA) which detects serum antibodies against *E. cuniculi*. Rabbits who have been exposed to *E. cuniculi* and cleared the infection or those with a latent infection may still have antibodies. Thus, a positive result only indicates that the rabbit has at some time been exposed to *E. cuniculi*, not necessarily that there is an active infection. To evaluate the course of the disease, Sound Diagnostics in Seattle, Washington (the lab which performs the *E. cuniculi* serologic test) suggests testing two samples collected 2 to 4 weeks apart. Based on data gathered from testing hundreds of samples, Sound Diagnostics has found the following:

1. Two negative samples indicate the rabbit is not currently infected.

2. Values that rise significantly over a 2 to 4 week period usually indicate the presence of an acute infection.

3. Low-positive values that remain stable and are not accompanied by symptoms indicate that the rabbit's immune system is keeping the infection under control.

4. High-positive values that are accompanied by typical signs of the disease indicate that the rabbit's immune system is unable to control the infection.

Many house rabbits test positive for *E. cuniculi*. Some live long, healthy lives without ever displaying symptoms while others exhibit symptoms when they experience something stressful such as an illness or loss of a mate. *E. cuniculi* infection can be kept in check by a rabbit's immune system. However, if the rabbit's health (mental or physical) is compromised, the rabbit may start to show signs of the disease.

Although the *E. cuniculi* serologic test has been around for several years, many rabbit caretakers were reluctant to have their rabbits tested, unless symptoms were present, because there was no known treatment. Although this information might have been useful in the treatment of seemingly unrelated problems, many of us simply didn't want to know that our treasured companions might have a "ticking timebomb".

If your veterinarian thinks your rabbit should be tested for *E. cuniculi*, have her contact Sound Diagnostics in Seattle, Washington for details. (Complete contact information is provided in the *Resources* section at the back of this book.) The lab will report back to your veterinarian with an optical density (O.D.) reading (often referred to loosely, but incorrectly, as the "titer") of the sample, and an interpretation of the O.D. number (e.g., positive or negative). The O.D. is proportional to the amount of *E. cuniculi* antibody in your rabbit's blood.

Treatment with Oxibendazole, Albendazole, or Fenbendazole

Many symptomatic rabbits have been treated with oxibendazole, a horse-worming paste that is inexpensive and can be purchased from veterinary supply companies without a prescription. However, as with all medications, treatment should be given under the supervision of a veterinarian. Most rabbits treated with oxibendazole have tolerated it well. A few rabbits have experienced mild side effects including either increased or decreased activity levels and slight decreases in appetite. Many symptomatic rabbits show some clinical improvement after two to three weeks or less and some completely recover. Others show no improvement until medication has been given for two to three months. Some are stable while on treatment and signs recur when treatment is discontinued. In some cases, treatment with oxibendazole has no apparent effect. Treatment with oxibendazole usually lasts for several months.

Some veterinarians prefer albendazole to oxibendazole. Albendazole is a drug used in humans to treat lesions caused by certain tapeworms. Because albendazole does not cross the blood/brain barrier as well as oxibendazole, it may be less effective, especially in cases where head tilt is the primary symptom.

A study published in the <u>Veterinary Record</u> (April 14, 2001, pp.478-480) suggests that fenbendazole, a drug used to treat pinworms, may be effective in both preventing and curing *E. cuniculi* infections. Based on this study, some veterinarians are now prescribing fenbendazole for rabbits with symptomatic *E. cuniculi*.

Your veterinarian will probably have a "first choice" treatment for symptomatic *E. cuniculi* based on her personal experience (good or bad) with one or more of the treatments. She will also consider your rabbit's symptoms and medical history, including his reaction to other medications. If your rabbit's condition continues to deteriorate after a reasonable time on one treatment, ask your veterinarian if she is open to trying one of the other treatments. There is still much that is unknown about this condition, and it is possible that different manifestations of symptoms respond to different treatments. It is also possible that individual rabbits will respond to one treatment and not another.

Oxibendazole, albendazole, and fenbendazole all may cause mild to moderate elevation of liver enzymes. While these values usually return to normal after the medication is discontinued, your veterinarian will want to do periodic blood tests to monitor liver enzyme levels.

Some veterinarians also recommend that you treat any rabbit who has been in contact with a rabbit being treated. You and your veterinarian should make this decision together, considering each individual rabbit's overall health and sensitivity to medications in general—as well as the rabbit's temperament and ease in administering medications (especially long term).

Other Treatments and Supportive Care for Symptomatic Rabbits

In addition to oxibendazole, albendazole, or fenbendazole, rabbits who exhibit symptoms may benefit from treatment with echinacea (an herb which boosts the immune system) and goldenseal. If symptoms include head-tilt, kidney disease, paralysis, or liver disease, refer to those sections of this book for additional treatment and supportive care ideas. Baytril, another commonly used rabbit medication, can provide improvement with the clinical signs of *E. cuniculi* although the exact mechanism for this improvement is not clearly understood. Finally, acupuncture can help in restoring harmony in the body and boosting the immune system.

Head Tilt

Head tilt (also known as torticollis or wry neck) is not a single disease. Instead, head tilt is a **symptom** of a variety of medical problems. In rabbits, the most common of these are:

- Middle-/inner-ear infections (bacterial)
- *E. cuniculi* infection

Head tilt can also be caused by stroke; cancer involving the head, neck, or ear; head trauma; raccoon or skunk round worms (*Baylisascaris* spp.); or poisoning. The tilt itself is caused by neurological damage, either temporary or permanent. It may be preceded by a brief period of general "unsteadiness" or a wobbly head. Your rabbit's chances of recovery are best if your veterinarian is able to correctly identify the underlying cause of the tilt. In many cases, however, diagnosis is difficult and may require advanced imaging techniques such as MRI or CT scans—techniques that are very expensive and may not be available. Early detection and aggressive treatment also improve your rabbit's chances for a quick and complete recovery.

Ear Infections

An outer-ear infection that is left untreated may work its way into the middle and inner ear, resulting in head tilt. If your rabbit shows signs of an ear infection—scratching his ears, excessive head shaking, or a "bump" at the base of his ear—consult your veterinarian immediately. Bacterial infections can occasionally **begin** in the inner ear.

Most ear infections produce a discharge that can be cultured to identify responsible bacteria and the antibiotic(s) to which it is sensitive. If no discharge is present, a skull x-ray **may** help confirm that the illness is caused by an inner-ear problem. However, not all middle or inner ear infections can be confirmed with an x-ray. Endoscopy is another diagnostic technique that allows a thorough exam of the external ear and tympanum (ear drum). Severe middle ear infections that may not show up on an x-ray can sometimes be detected with this technique.

If an ear infection appears to be the cause of the illness and there is no discharge to culture, most veterinarians will choose to treat with the antibiotic(s) that have worked well for them in the past. Many veterinarians will begin by prescribing two antibiotics (from two different classes) that are known to have a synergistic effect. If an outer-ear infection is also present, your veterinarian will probably prescribe ear drops along with systemic antibiotics.

Antibiotic treatment for head-tilt needs to be aggressive and prolonged. If no improvement is noticed after two or three weeks, your veterinarian will most likely change antibiotics or add an additional one. Once an effective antibiotic (or combination) is found, long-term treatment (at least two weeks after symptoms are greatly improved or resolved) is usually necessary. In some cases your rabbit may need to remain on antibiotics indefinitely to prevent recurrence. Severe infections may cause permanent damage to a rabbit's balance sensing system and some tilt may remain even though the infection is completely cured.

E. Cuniculi

E. cuniculi is a parasitic infection that affects the brain, central nervous system, and other vital organs. The head tilt in *E. cuniculi* bunnies results from brain damage caused by the parasites and may be the result of an active stage of the disease or permanent neurological damage. Although there is currently no cure for this disease, in many cases it can be successfully controlled for several years. Diagnosis and treatment of *E. cuniculi* is discussed in detail in the previous section of this chapter.

Managing Symptoms and Providing Supportive Care

It is important to properly diagnose the cause of head-tilt and begin appropriate medication to cure or control the underlying disease. It is equally important to manage the symptoms, keeping the bunny as comfortable as possible during treatment of the disease.

The following medical treatments have proven helpful to head-tilt bunnies, independent of the cause of the tilt:

- If the "down" eye (the one facing the floor) is not able to close, eye ointment or liquid tears will help keep it moist.

- Lactated Ringers Solution (LRS) can be administered subcutaneously to keep your rabbit hydrated and to keep electrolytes in balance.

- Meclizine (Antivert®) can help relieve dizziness and restore appetite.

- Short-term steroids or anti-inflammatories may speed recovery by reducing inflammation and may improve appetite by reducing pain. Steroids such as prednisone are known to suppress the immune system, so non-steroidal anti-inflammatories (NSAIDS) such as Rimadyl® or ibuprofen may be a better choice, especially if your rabbit has a bacterial infection.

- Acupuncture may help reduce symptoms, restore balance, and improve overall health.

Discuss these possibilities with your veterinarian to see which might be helpful to your rabbit.

It is impossible to overstate the value of **supportive care** in helping bunnies overcome head tilt or any other serious ailment. The presence of a loving caretaker who nurses him through the difficulties of eating, drinking, moving, and keeping clean are critical to maintaining a bunny's "fighting" spirit. The strength of a bunny's desire to recover and will to live are just as important to his recovery as proper medical care.

The chapter titled *Providing Intensive Care* contains many suggestions about supportive care that will make life easier for bunnies with head-tilt as well as many other disabling conditions. The following are some additional suggestions specifically aimed at making a head-tilt bunny more comfortable:

- Lack of balance may cause your rabbit to "roll" or have difficulty standing. He may do better in a smaller space—a cage, pen, padded dog bed, or box with high sides. Consider placing him in an area that is quiet, yet close to family activities so he does not feel isolated and lonely. Be sure there is padding on all sides of his area and around all hard surfaces such as food and water bowls.

  Pillows, foam-rubber pieces in various shapes and sizes, or rolled towels and baby blankets can be used for padding and to prop your rabbit up. You'll need to experiment to see what works best for an individual rabbit. Foam rubber should be covered with sturdy fabric so the rabbit can't tear it apart—don't worry, he won't critique your sewing skills! Make sure towels and blankets are rolled tightly and secured so your rabbit cannot get tangled in them when he rolls. You can use large safety pins to keep towels/blankets from unrolling, but be **sure** to keep pins safely out of your rabbit's reach. Heavy-duty Velcro is another option. Anchor all padding as securely as you can to the side of the cage or box by threading thin wire (or long twist-ties) through the padding and, if necessary, the enclosure and twisting it securely on the side away from the rabbit.

- If your rabbit is mobile enough to still be able to use a litter-box, make his life easier by providing one with at least one low side for easy entry. Otherwise, line his area with a synthetic sheepskin rug that allows urine to pass through but will keep the rabbit dry. Have several of these on hand and wash them frequently.

- Picking up head-tilt bunnies **may** increase their vertigo. If this seems to be the case with your rabbit, try to minimize the number of times you pick him up (e.g., give medications and other care that requires handling at the same time instead of picking him up multiple times). In other cases rabbits—even ones who normally hate to be held—have been known to completely relax when cradled like a baby, often drifting off into much-needed sleep. When picking up a head-tilt rabbit, hold him securely against your own body to help him feel as stable as possible. If he seems to enjoy it, spend as much time as you can holding him.

Head tilt is usually a long-term illness—don't expect a miraculous recovery overnight. In the early stages of treatment, symptoms often become much worse before getting better. Try not to get discouraged and don't give up prematurely. Some rabbits have recovered after a year of combined drug and acupuncture therapy. You, as the caretaker, may have a harder time adjusting to your bunny's new appearance than he has adjusting to his handicap. Aggressive medical care, in conjunction with a loving and supportive environment, can provide your rabbit with a good quality of life even if your rabbit has some permanent neurological damage.

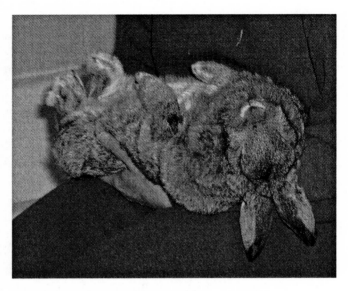

*Henrietta developed head-tilt just before Christmas 2001. Her initial symptoms were a slightly wobbly head and unsteadiness on her feet. The tilt did not actually develop until **after** her visit to the vet! Thanks to early detection and aggressive treatment, her tilt was hardly noticeable after two weeks of treatment and today she is completely back to normal. Even while she was ill, Henrietta enjoyed being cradled like a baby. When I cleaned her area, I cradled her with my left arm and cleaned with my right.* (Photo by Sue Bergstrand.)

Bladder Sludge

Bladder sludge may be triggered by a bladder or urinary tract infection, by an inability to completely empty the bladder because of an arthritic condition, or by excess calcium in the urine. While bladder stones are large masses of this excess calcium, sludge consists of many crystals the size of a grain of sand or smaller. Humans and most other domestic animals absorb digestible calcium from their diets based on the body's needs at the time. However, rabbits seem to absorb calcium in proportion to the amount present in their diet. Excess calcium is excreted in the urine, giving a cloudy appearance to the urine. It is not unusual for a healthy rabbit's urine to be cloudy at times.

Factors that **may** lead to bladder sludge include:

1.　**Diet high in digestible calcium.** The most common culprits are alfalfa hay and pellets with high calcium contents. Usually, removing these from the diet is sufficient. Although some vegetables are higher than others in calcium, these calcium levels are low compared to alfalfa hay and most pellets. You only want to reduce the amount of calcium in the diet, not eliminate it completely!

2.　**Insufficient water intake.** This results in more concentrated urine and less frequent urination. If your rabbit drinks very little from a water bottle, try giving water in a heavy crock instead. Often rabbits will drink more water from a bowl than from a bottle. Adding a small amount of **unsweetened** fruit juice to the water may also encourage him to drink more.

3.　**Obesity/Inactivity.** An active rabbit will drink more and therefore urinate more frequently. Exercise also helps burn calories. Provide plenty of room for exercise and a variety of toys to stimulate activity. An active companion will often encourage a sedate rabbit to get more exercise.

4.　**Inadequate toilet facilities.** Observe your rabbit's toilet habits. If he refuses to go in a soiled litter-box, try to clean it more frequently. If he refuses to go while in his cage, try to minimize cage time or purchase a larger cage so he has room for a bathroom **and** a "living area."

5.   **Arthritic conditions.** Spondylosis and other arthritic conditions may cause a rabbit to be unable to completely empty his bladder because he cannot get in the correct position.

6.   **Genetic predisposition.** The most important factor in the development of sludge may be the individual rabbit's metabolism and how his body handles calcium. Some rabbits develop sludge even with a caretaker who does all the right things!

Symptoms

Bladder sludge may be difficult to recognize in its early stages. It is not unusual for a rabbit's urine to occasionally be an opaque white and for there to be some white chalky material in the litter-box. However, frequent creamy white urine may be a caretaker's first sign that a rabbit is in danger of developing bladder sludge. If this occurs and you have not already done so, reduce the calcium in your rabbit's diet by switching from alfalfa to timothy hay; reduce the amount of pellets you feed; and ensure that you are using pellets with a calcium level of <1%.

As the condition progresses, symptoms of sludge **may** include:

1.   Loss of litter-box habits, including dribbling of urine.

2.   Urine that is a thick, white, toothpaste-like consistency.

3.   Straining to urinate. If he is straining to urinate, your rabbit may sit in the litter-box for a long time with his tail held high in the air. In many cases, very little urine may be produced. Occasionally, your rabbit may cry or moan in pain while straining. If your rabbit strains and produces **no** urine, get him to a vet immediately—this may be an emergency!

Diagnosis

Sludge is normally diagnosed by some combination of the following:

1.   **Physical Examination.** Signs of sludge may be detected during a physical exam for an unrelated problem. A sludge-filled bladder may feel doughy when palpated or be painful. Other outward signs of sludge may include small crystals accumulated around the rabbit's tail.

2.   **Urinalysis.** A urinalysis provides information about the chemical composition of the urine, including amount of calcium present and

existing infections/inflammation. Bladder sludge may or may not be accompanied by a urinary tract infection. However, chronic sludge problems may irritate and damage the bladder wall, making your rabbit more susceptible to frequent or chronic bladder infections.

As it is unlikely that you can convince your rabbit to produce a urine sample in a cup, you may wonder how to obtain a urine sample from him. Four methods are described below—one of the last two must be used if a sterile sample is required:

- **Free catch.** You may be able to obtain a urine sample yourself. Empty the litter-box (no newspaper, litter, or hay), clean thoroughly, and wait for your rabbit to urinate. Collect a sample immediately using a syringe or eye-dropper and store in a clean plastic or glass container. It is best to get the sample to your vet as soon as possible; however, the sample may be refrigerated for up to eight hours. Often, this is the least stressful way to collect a urine sample. However, if your rabbit is part of a group and you have to separate him from his companions, this method may actually be more stressful than the other methods described. Also, be aware that some rabbits may not urinate in a litter-box without litter.

- **Manual expression.** If your rabbit is cooperative and has a full bladder, a skilled veterinarian or technician may be able to obtain a sample by gently massaging the bladder, causing your rabbit to urinate. Getting the rabbit to urinate is only half the battle—the other half is directing the urine into a collection cup.

- **Cystocentesis.** A sterile sample can be collected by inserting a small needle into the bladder through the abdominal wall and extracting a urine sample. This process can be completed in a few seconds with only minor discomfort. Depending on your rabbit's temperament, this procedure may not require anesthesia. **Note: Only an experienced rabbit veterinarian should perform this procedure.**

- **Catheterization.** Another way to collect a sterile sample is by threading a small, soft catheter into the bladder via the urethra and extracting a urine sample. There is some risk of causing or worsening an existing infection by transporting bacteria into the bladder on the catheter. Thus, only an experienced rabbit veterinarian should perform this procedure.

Be sure to mention to your veterinarian if you have a rabbit like my Murray who is especially "uncooperative" about giving a urine sample (Murray often empties his bladder in the carrier on the way to the vet). Most veterinarians **do** routinely feel the bladder to make sure urine is present **before** trying to obtain a sample. If the bladder is empty and your veterinarian feels it is important to get a urine sample, she may suggest giving sub-q fluids, waiting until the bladder fills, and then obtaining a sample.

3.   **X-ray.** Because sludge is composed primarily of calcium, it should be easily detectable on an x-ray, appearing as white areas. It is not unusual for normal rabbits to have some small amount of this material present in their bladders. Pea or grape-sized dense masses often indicate the presence of stones. Sludge often appears as an opaque area, often filling half or even the entire bladder.

4.   **Ultrasound.** Ultrasound is another diagnostic means of looking at the internal organs. It often gives more detailed information on specific organs such as the kidneys.

5.   **Blood Work.** Laboratory analysis of the blood—discussed in detail in a later chapter—usually consists of Serum Chemistry tests and Complete Blood Cell Count (CBC). Serum Chemistry tests indicate the condition of vital organs such as the kidneys and liver and will also give a blood calcium level. CBC tests indicate the overall health of the rabbit, including signs of infection and presence of conditions such as anemia.

Treatment

While bladder stones nearly always require surgical removal, most cases of sludge do not require surgery unless there is a blockage. Non-surgical treatments include:

1.   **Flushing the bladder.** To flush the bladder, your veterinarian will probably catheterize your bunny and gently introduce saline into the bladder to dilute the sludge. The diluted sludge is then suctioned out into a syringe and the process is repeated as many times as necessary. This process sometimes requires anesthesia, depending on the severity of the sludge.

2. **Increasing fluid intake.** Fluid intake can be increased by giving subcu-
    taneous fluids, by syringe feeding oral fluids, or by simply tempting
    your rabbit to drink more. A rabbit can sometimes be tempted to
    drink more by adding small amounts of natural fruit juice (no added
    sugar) to the drinking water. If you are syringe-feeding oral fluids, you
    may want to try a variety of juices (pineapple, grape, apple, and
    cherry) or nectars (apricot, peach, and pear) to see which ones your
    rabbit takes willingly. Start with 2/3 water and 1/3 juice, and gradually
    reduce the amount of juice. **Caution:** If your rabbit has companions,
    provide a separate water source for the companions—just in case they
    dislike the flavor you are adding to the water!

3. **Analgesics.** Analgesics (pain relievers) may be prescribed to relieve
    discomfort caused by catheterization or to relieve potential back pain
    and allow for a more normal urination posture. How long medication
    is needed will depend on the procedure performed and the individual
    rabbit's tolerance of pain. When your rabbit is urinating normally,
    moving around comfortably, and eating well, try discontinuing the
    pain medicine. If pain returns when medication is withdrawn, consult
    your veterinarian about continuing it, perhaps at a lower dose.

4. **Vitamin C/Cranberry.** Vitamin C can help heal urinary tract tissue
    that has been damaged or irritated by catheterization. Cranberry is a
    good source of Vitamin C and studies in humans have shown that
    cranberry actually helps prevent bladder infections. Use cranberry
    tablets or 100% cranberry juice—cranberry juice cocktail contains
    lots of sugar and very little cranberry juice!

5. **Antibiotics.** If the urinalysis indicates an infection, your veterinarian
    will probably start your rabbit on an antibiotic and suggest doing a cul-
    ture/sensitivity test to confirm that the antibiotic chosen will be effec-
    tive. Depending on the overall health of your rabbit and the amount of
    trauma your vet feels catheterization caused, she may prescribe antibi-
    otic therapy even if no infection was indicated by the urinalysis. For
    severe or recurrent urinary tract infections, antibiotics may need to be
    given for six to eight weeks. Your veterinarian will probably suggest that
    the urinalysis be repeated a week or two after your rabbit completes
    antibiotic treatment to confirm the infection is cured.

6. **Phenoxybenzamine and Bethanechol.** Some veterinarians prescribe
    drugs such as phenoxybenzamine and bethanechol to aid in relaxing

the sphincter, controlling the outflow of urine from the bladder, or increasing muscular contractions and emptying of the bladder.

Note: Urinary acidifiers, often prescribed for cats with bladder stones, should not be prescribed for rabbits. Rabbits are herbivores and their urine is normally alkaline. Products designed to make the urine more acidic will not work and may actually do harm!

Long-Term Implications

Rabbits who have had bladder sludge frequently have recurrences of the problem. Changes made to reduce calcium in the diet, increase fluid intake, and encourage exercise need to be permanent lifestyle changes for your rabbit. You will want to watch your rabbit carefully and consult your veterinarian at the first sign that sludge is returning. As with most rabbit conditions, the earlier it is caught, the easier it is to treat. Finally, your veterinarian may suggest regular checkup visits—please follow her recommendations!

Among his many physical problems, Murray occasionally suffers mild attacks of sludge. Here, His Royal Highness inspects the low-calcium organic greens just purchased by his faithful servant to ensure they are up to his standards before they go into his refrigerator. (Photo by Kathy Smith)

Abscesses

An abscess is defined as a collection of pus that is localized by a zone of inflamed tissue. Abscesses can be visible and accessible externally or a mass (which might be a tumor or an abscess) may be detected on an x-ray. Diagnosis and treatment of an abscess depends on its size and location.

Abscesses can occur almost anywhere and can have a number of causes including (but not limited to):

• External puncture wounds

• Food impacted alongside the tooth or in longitudinal tooth fractures

• Systemic infections resulting in abscesses

Abscesses in rabbits are particularly hard to cure. They require persistent and aggressive treatment. Even with the best treatment by a skilled veterinarian, the recurrence rate is very high.

Treatment of abscesses in rabbits is more difficult than in other species for the following reasons:

• Pus in rabbits is **very** thick, making it difficult, if not impossible, to drain the abscess. The consistency of rabbit pus is often likened to cream cheese or toothpaste.

• Rabbits tend to wall off abscesses, preventing or limiting appropriate antibiotic levels from being reached within the abscess.

• Rabbit abscesses often form finger-like extensions, making the abscesses **much** larger than original appearances. These "fingers" often make the abscess difficult to remove completely.

• The number of relatively safe antibiotics is much smaller for rabbits than for most other species, limiting treatment options.

Treatment of an abscess depends on its location and size. Surgical removal is usually indicated unless the abscess is located where it cannot be easily accessed, where its removal might endanger vital organs, or if the rabbit's general health is too compromised for surgery. The steps normally taken to treat an abscess include:

1.   Surgically remove the entire abscess, including the capsule and all extensions. Surrounding tissue (sometimes bone) may also need to be removed to ensure removal of all the infection.

2.   Collect a sample of the capsule wall (not the pus itself, which is usually sterile) and submit for culture and sensitivity. It is critical to identify the pathogen that caused the abscess and the antibiotics that will be effective against it.

3.   Clean the area thoroughly.

4.   Depending on the location of the abscess, your veterinarian may pack the area with antibiotic beads or medicated gel foam.

5.   The wound is often left open allowing the area to heal from the inside out. Some veterinarians accomplish this by suturing the wound shut around a drain. Others use a wet-to-dry dextrose bandage (which must be changed daily) to pack the wound and keep it from closing.

6.   Rabbits are usually put on systemic antibiotics for weeks or months following abscess surgery. The antibiotic is normally started immediately after surgery and changed if necessary when the culture and sensitivity results are available.

7.   Depending on the location of the abscess, you may need to perform daily cleaning or flushing of the area. It is critical that you diligently follow your veterinarian's instructions even though the procedure may be stressful for both you and your rabbit.

If your veterinarian feels that surgery is not an option, either because of the location of the abscess or because of your rabbit's general health, she may choose to simply try antibiotic treatment. If possible, she will probably try to obtain a sample for culture and sensitivity to improve the probability that the antibiotic will be effective. Bicillin (a combination of two forms of penicillin-G) has been successful in treating many abscesses that could not safely be removed surgically or cultured or in some cases limiting further growth. Note, however, that bicillin will only be an effective treatment if the abscess is caused by a type of bacteria that is sensitive to penicillin. The bicillin treatment protocol is available online at

http://moorelab.sbs.umass.edu/~mrosenfield/bicillin/

Another technique that has been successfully used when surgery wasn't an option is to inject a low dose of antibiotics such as gentamicin or amikacin directly into the abscess. Again, this treatment will only work if the abscess is caused by bacteria that is sensitive to the antibiotic used.

Curing an abscess requires diligent care from both you and your veterinarian. You may want to ask your veterinarian to outline a complete treatment plan. If there is any part of the plan that you don't understand or have concerns about—or if important steps (e.g. culture and sensitivity tests) are missing from the plan, speak up. If you are not comfortable with the treatment plan, ask your veterinarian if she would consult with one of the experts listed in the *Resources* section before proceeding—or seek a second opinion yourself.

Samson and Xena enjoyed each other's company throughout Samson's long battle with jaw abscesses. (Photo by Kristi Cole)

Arthritis/Spondylosis

Arthritis is an inflammatory condition of the joints characterized by pain and swelling. In animals, as in humans, the amount of discomfort and disability varies from day to day and can be affected by a combination of factors including temperature, humidity, barometric pressure, and recent activity levels.

Spondylosis is a degenerative condition of the spine. In early stages of the disease, the vertebrae in the back gradually develop "spurs" which may rub against each other causing pain. As the disease progresses, these spurs eventually bridge together, fusing the vertebrae and decreasing the spine's flexibility. As they degenerate, the vertebra may also pinch nerves causing pain and/or musculoskeletal weakness. Spondylosis is fairly common in rabbits over four years of age and is most common in medium– to large–breed females, especially the obese. As with arthritis, the symptoms vary from day to day and are affected by weather and activity levels.

Both arthritis and spondylosis can be diagnosed with x-rays. They have been grouped together because symptomatic treatments, physical therapy techniques, and supportive care requirements are similar for the two diseases.

Symptomatic Treatment

For both arthritis and spondylosis, the primary goal is to control pain and keep the bunny mobile without creating GI problems. When considering the GI risks of pain medications and steroids, it is important to also remember that immobility itself can trigger an attack of GI stasis.

Finding the right medication and dosage for your rabbit will probably require some trial and error. As with humans, each individual rabbit has a different tolerance for pain and a different response to each drug. Non-steroidal anti-inflammatory drugs (NSAIDS) decrease swelling and inflammation in addition to reducing pain. NSAIDS that are frequently used to treat the pain of arthritis or spondylosis include:

- Aspirin
- Ibuprofen
- Rimadyl® (carprofen)
- Metacam® (meloxicam)

Although the first two are available without a prescription, you should work closely with your veterinarian to determine the best dosage for your rabbit and to monitor side effects.

In some cases, your veterinarian may suggest treating the arthritis or spondylosis with a steroid such as dexamethasone or prednisone **instead** of an NSAID. Many NSAIDs should not be used along with steroids because both may cause GI upset. Be sure your veterinarian is aware of all medications, prescription and non-prescription, that your rabbit is taking.

Veterinarians have used both Adequan® (polysulfated glycosaminoglycan) injections and Cosequin® tablets (glucosamine with chondroiten) to help manage symptoms of many degenerative joint conditions in rabbits. While glucosamine/chondroiten is available without a prescription, be sure to consult your veterinarian before using this product.

Acupuncture has also been effective in relieving pain in rabbits with arthritis and spondylosis. If pain medication doesn't seem to be working—or if you are more comfortable trying holistic treatments for pain—see if there is a veterinary acupuncturist in your area who is knowledgeable about rabbits or is willing to learn about them.

Regularly applying heat or giving a gentle massage to the **muscles** around the painful area can help your rabbit relax. If your rabbit enjoys it, massage can be a wonderful way to communicate love and support while giving physical comfort. Heat lamps or radiant space heaters can also help with pain relief. Be sure these are out of your rabbit's reach and remember to bunny-proof the electrical cords.

Finally, if your rabbit is obese, reducing his weight will help reduce the load on the back and joints. This alone can significantly reduce the pain associated with arthritis or spondylosis.

Physical Therapy

You should do everything you can to encourage your rabbit to exercise. If he has trouble moving and/or supporting his weight, you may need to use some creativity to help him remain mobile. If your rabbit is making an effort to move but is having trouble standing or using his legs, try making a sling out of a narrow towel and use this to hold him upright. In many cases, this gentle support will encourage your rabbit to move his legs. You may be amazed at how well he is able to move around with some support (both physical and moral) from you.

If you are resourceful (and handy), you may want to try building a scooter or cart to help your rabbit get around without as much help from you. You can also order custom-built carts from the companies listed under "Special Needs Supplies" in the *Resources* section at the end of this book. By keeping your rabbit mobile, you improve his outlook on life, keep his muscles toned, and keep the GI moving!

Supportive Care

Supportive care consists of observing your rabbit's daily activities, identifying things that are becoming difficult for him, and finding a way to make them easier or do them for him. In some cases it may also mean making adjustments in your life so he can still feel like a part of the family. Some examples include:

- If your rabbit has trouble hopping into the litter-box, make one side lower so he can easily step in.

- If your rabbit is having trouble hopping into his cage or up on his favorite "perch" (table, chair, window seat, etc.), build him a ramp. Start with a piece of wood long enough so the ramp isn't too steep. Cover it with carpet so your bunny's feet don't slip, and fasten it securely to the cage or favorite "perch."

- If you have a multi-level home and your bunny can no longer go up and down stairs, you could always move to a one-level house! Too drastic? Then try moving all of your bunny's things to one floor— preferably the one where you and your family spend the most time— and take care to restrict his access to stairs.

- If your rabbit has weakness in the hind limbs, he may not be able to keep his ears clean. Check his ears at least weekly for excess wax accumulation, and clean them for him if necessary.

- If your rabbit has trouble sitting up on his own, foam rubber pieces of various shapes and sizes can be arranged to prop him up comfortably.

- If your rabbit can only move within a small area, you will need to move all of his things—litter-box, food, water, hay, toys, etc.—to one place. This should be the part of your house where your family spends the most time—even if that means having a litter-box and hay in your family room! It is important for your rabbit to know he is still an important part of your family.

Loss of Mobility

Rabbits may lose mobility from a number of diseases and conditions:

- Arthritis/Spondylosis
- Back or spinal injury
- *E. cuniculi*
- Infections other than *E. cuniculi*
- Neurological ailments of unknown origin
- Stroke
- Birth Defects

Some of these conditions cause paralysis of one or more limbs while others make movement painful. Depending on the cause of the impaired movement, some rabbits may regain partial or even complete mobility given time, appropriate medications, physical therapy, and lots of TLC.

Rabbits who lose mobility in their hind-quarters require special care. They are often unable to get into a litter-box or even move away from a urine-soaked area. This often leads to serious problems with urine scald and a messy bottom and underside. A synthetic sheepskin rug will allow urine to pass through but will keep the bunny dry. In extreme cases, your veterinarian might recommend diapering your rabbit. If you feel your rabbit needs to be diapered, please discuss the pros and cons with your veterinarian before proceeding and have her show you the proper technique. In cases of neurological injury, your rabbit may not be able to empty his bladder and may require short- or long-term help emptying his bladder. Your veterinarian can show you how to do this.

If your rabbit's loss of mobility is not due to a recent back injury and he is able to move at all, encourage him to exercise. (Moving around should be discouraged in a rabbit recovering from a back injury.) As mentioned in the section on *Arthritis/Spondylosis*, try making a sling out of a narrow towel and use this to hold him upright. If he is able to move with this support, you may want to discuss with your veterinarian whether a scooter or cart might help him—such devices give some rabbits a whole new lease on life. Caretakers who are resourceful (and handy) have built scooters and other "mobility devices" which enable their handicapped rabbits to get around quite well and eliminate the urine scald and messy bottom problems. For those of us who are not so handy, carts can also be ordered from K-9 Cart Co. or Doggon' Wheels.

Contact information for these companies is included in the *Resources* section at the end of the book. Carts are custom-built for each animal—you will probably want your veterinarian to help make sure measurements are as accurate as possible.

While many caretakers choose to euthanize when mobility becomes a problem, others recognize an incredible strength and will to live in their rabbit at this point. Rabbits can still have good quality of life despite mobility problems.

In February 2002 Ebony, a splay-legged black lop joined my family. X-rays show he suffers from the shoulder equivalent of hip dysplasia. He has adjusted remarkably well to his handicap with the help of his bonded companion Ivory. (Photo by Darice Heishman)

Blindness

If you suspect your bunny is blind—or is going blind—the first step is to consult a veterinarian to see if there is an underlying disease that needs to be treated. For example, cataracts are usually just a sign of aging. They can also result from trauma, an underlying genetic predisposition, or *E. cuniculi*. Depending on what your veterinarian suspects, she may suggest blood work to rule out *E. cuniculi* and other conditions, head x-rays to check for tumors and abscesses, or other diagnostic tests. If you have access to a veterinary ophthalmologist, your veterinarian may suggest a consultation to rule out glaucoma and to discuss treatment options.

If your rabbit is blind because of cataracts, you may wonder about surgery. This is a personal decision that should be made by you, your veterinarian(s), and your rabbit. When Choca Paws developed cataracts at age six, we discussed this option with a veterinary ophthalmologist. We were told that the procedure was very expensive and that there was no guarantee that it would be successful. More importantly, the surgeon had no prior experience with rabbits and we would have to take Choca Paws (who hated car rides) two hours each way for the procedure. I asked the ophthalmologist if he recommended the procedure. His answer was that he always felt that cataract surgery in animals was more for the owner than for the animal. This frank response helped me feel comfortable with our decision not to subject Choca Paws to surgery.

If you determine that your bunny is permanently blind, the first thing to remember is that rabbits are not nearly as dependent on their eyesight as we humans are. A blind bunny can live quite happily with only a few minor adjustments.

A blind bunny's main living area—including placement of his litter-box, food, and water—should stay as consistent as possible. A roomy bathroom, partitioned off by a baby gate, is ideal because the fixtures tend to stay put. It is also a room that humans visit frequently, so the bunny will have plenty of human interaction.

A blind bunny will still want to explore beyond the limits of his area. Make sure you are there to help if he gets into trouble. When Choca Paws came out to explore the rest of the house, he ran rather awkwardly, keeping his nose to the ground most of the time. Sometimes he got overly confident about remembering where things were and ran (sometimes hard) into a piece of furniture or wall (usually something that was **always** there, not something that was moved recently). It never really slowed him down. I think it hurt my husband and me more to see him run into something than it hurt him.

If your bunny doesn't have a mate and has been neutered (or you are comfortable having him neutered), consider getting him a **gentle** mate of the opposite sex. Having a companion of his own species can be a great comfort for a disabled bunny, and you can learn a lot about compassion by watching a bunny look after his mate. If you decide to consider a mate, arrange with the nearest rescue group or shelter to bring your blind bunny along and let him help pick out his companion. This will improve the chances of a low-stress bonding experience. Carefully observe your bunny's interactions with his potential mate and listen to your instincts—they will help you know whether your blind bunny will be happier alone or with a rabbit companion.

Remember, sight is only one of the five senses. Stimulate the others, especially hearing and touch. Always speak (softly) as you approach a blind bunny, so as not to startle him. Spend as much time as you can with him—sit next to him, pet him, and speak soothingly to him. Since he can't see you, touch lets him know you are near and that you love him. If you are lucky, like we were with Choca Paws, he will reward you with "bunny kisses." Try not to pick a blind bunny up any more than necessary unless you are certain he enjoys it. Being lifted off the ground is threatening to many bunnies and can be even more frightening to one who cannot see.

You will continue to learn how your bunny adapts to his handicap—and you will be amazed at how intelligent he is. About a week after Smokey died of cancer, Choca Paws ventured into the kitchen (Smokey's "private space") for the first time ever. I heard this incessant tippity-tap, tippity-tap, tippity-tap—the kitchen is decent sized, but not huge. Finally, I got up to see what he was doing. He was going back and forth along one wall—over and over. I said, "What **are** you doing?" Then I realized...he was "learning" the dimensions of this new room. At that moment, I was overwhelmed with the depth of this brave creature's intelligence and ability to adapt.

 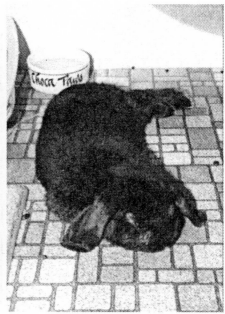

Choca Paws as a young bunny.
(Photo by Kathy Smith)

Choca Paws after he lost his sight.
(Photo by Kathy Smith)

Deafness

Many people assume their rabbit is deaf—or at least hearing-impaired—if he seems to startle easily. Remember, rabbits are prey animals and must stay alert to stay alive in many situations; therefore they often startle easily. Although we hope our companion rabbits feel safe in our care, occasionally a noise, sight, or sound that goes unnoticed by humans will trigger an instinctive "alert" response. The specific stimuli that trigger these responses will be determined, in large part, by the experiences your rabbit had before coming to the safety of your care.

Others assume their rabbits are deaf because they do not react to loud noises such as the vacuum cleaner, a door slamming, or something falling on the floor. Not all bunnies will be afraid of noises.

Some indications that your rabbit may actually be deaf include:

•   Does not startle or react to loud noises that are not accompanied by excessive vibration (e.g., loud clattering of dishes), but **does** startle or react to noises that are accompanied by vibration (e.g., something heavy falling on the floor).

•   No response at all to **any** voice.

Note that although rabbits often react visibly to the sound of their primary caretaker's voice, some do not. They may hear (and understand) what you are saying to them, and simply choose to ignore you!

A rabbit may be deaf from birth or may become deaf as the result of a severe ear infection or other disease or injury. If you notice a sudden change in your rabbit's ability to hear, have him checked by a veterinarian immediately.

As mentioned in the section on blindness, if you determine your bunny is deaf, remember that hearing is only one of the five senses and your bunny doesn't need to hear in order to be safe. You will need to adjust how you communicate with your bunny, concentrating on the other four senses. Some suggestions include:

- Spend as much time as possible on the floor with your bunny. While this is important for all bunnies, it is especially important in gaining the trust of a deaf bunny.

- Go nose-to-nose as often as possible. This allows him to get used to both your sight and your scent.

- Beware of drastic changes in appearance. Even bunnies who can hear have been terrified by seemingly simple things such as suddenly seeing "mom," who always wears pants, in a full skirt! White apparel seems to be particularly scary to rabbits, perhaps because with white it is more difficult for them to recognize outlines.

- Avoid wearing perfume or using cosmetics (including shampoo and crème rinse) with a strong scent. You want your bunny to be used to your scent, not one from a bottle.

- If you have been eating meat or drinking milk, brush your teeth before going nose-to-nose with your bunny. The smell of animal products on your breath may make you smell like a predator.

- Make **brief** eye contact, then look away. Looking a long time is a challenge and may make your bunny see you as a predator.

- Learn to purr. Bunnies purr, and it is one of the few ways you can "sound like" a rabbit to a deaf rabbit. Once the bunny trusts you enough to let you do this, put your chin **gently** on his head, brush his head with your cheek or chin to imitate the grooming of a rabbit. Click your teeth together rapidly, or move your jaws back and forth rapidly to make a rattling sound like purring.

- Whenever possible, approach your bunny so he can see you coming. Try not to sneak up on your bunny from behind. Remember, he can't hear you coming (though he may sense the approach by the vibration of the floor).

Like all special needs bunnies, your deaf bunny will appreciate the efforts you make to help him adjust to his handicap.

As a baby, Sinbad displayed her musical talents. At age four, her mom discovered she was deaf when a stack of pot-and-pan lids fell out of the cabinet next to her—and Sinbad didn't flinch. Veterinary tests showed she was deaf and probably had been from birth. Sinbad's mom learned to communicate using light and scent. Despite being deaf, Sinbad was a very vocal bunny. (Photo by Cindy Scheel)

Kidney Disease

If your bunny has urinary tract symptoms, your veterinarian may suspect kidney disease—especially if your rabbit is elderly or symptoms are accompanied by weight loss. A diagnosis of kidney disease is normally confirmed with blood work, x-rays, and/or urinalysis. Note: Renal disease may not show up in blood work until 75% of the kidney is affected.

A urinalysis will often catch renal disease when about 66% of the kidney is affected. A mid-range specific gravity value (1.008–1.012) is one of the earliest indicators of kidney failure, especially when this value occurs in repeated samples. This may be accompanied by an increase in the amount of protein in the urine, indicating protein loss throughout the body. Casts collected in urine sediment can further help to differentiate the specific site or type of kidney disease.

If kidney disease is suspected and the urinalysis with culture/sensitivity rules out a urinary tract infection, your veterinarian will probably suggest x-rays to see if the kidneys have stones, are abnormally sized (enlarged or shrunken), or if bladder stones or sludge are present. She will probably also want to do a complete blood panel (both CBC and serum chemistry). The following tests are looked at most closely when kidney disease is suspected:

- Red Blood Cell Count (RBC)
- Creatinine
- Blood Urea Nitrogen (BUN)
- Serum calcium
- Serum phosphorus
- Serum potassium

If your rabbit has not already had an *E. cuniculi* titer, you may want to request one; *E. cuniculi* is a common cause of kidney disease. If the titer comes back positive, ask your veterinarian about treatment with oxibendozole, albendazole, or fenbendazole, all of which have shown promise in the treatment of *E. cuniculi*.

Your veterinarian may suggest syringe feeding one or more of the following to maintain weight:

- Oxbow's Critical Care (available only through veterinarians)

- Pellet "slurry" (ground pellets mixed with water)
- Canned pumpkin (be sure to get 100% pumpkin, not pie filling with spices)
- Ensure Lite dietary supplement (try strawberry flavor)
- Deliver 2.0 (available through pharmacies), which has a higher calorie content than Ensure and contains no sugar.

You may also want to try **small** amounts of oats and bread to help with weight maintenance. Your veterinarian can help you decide which of the above would be best for your rabbit, based on his general health and medical history. You may need to experiment—under your veterinarian's supervision—to see what your rabbit likes best and causes the least amount of GI upset.

Other supportive treatments you may want to discuss with your veterinarian include:

- Sub-q Fluids (requires a prescription and training from your veterinarian)
- Dandelion tincture (available at health food stores)
- Milk Thistle (available at health food stores)
- Lactulose (requires a prescription from your veterinarian)

Milk thistle and lactulose both help take ammonia from the blood and are a tonic for the liver which may also be compromised. Be sure to consult your veterinarian before using any non-prescription or herbal product.

If the RBC is sufficiently low, your veterinarian may prescribe Epogen® injections (erythropoietin) to help boost the RBC count—if not, you may want to ask her about this. Epogen can be obtained (by prescription only) from human pharmacies.

High creatinine and/or BUN levels can lead to stomach ulcers which may in turn cause the GI system to shut down completely. Sucralfate (a human ulcer treatment) has been successfully used on several rabbits, including my Goldie whose ulcers were discovered during GI surgery. Sucralfate binds to the ulcerated sites to form a protective barrier along the stomach/intestinal lining. It should be given twice a day for at least three to four weeks. **Note:** It is extremely important not to miss a dose, since Sucralfate works cumulatively. Sucralfate is most effective when given on an empty stomach. For a rabbit, try giving the drug about an hour before you would normally give him his fresh greens and, if possible, try to keep him from eating during that hour.

As with all conditions discussed in this chapter, a rabbit with kidney disease will have good days and bad days. Treasure the good ones and try not to get discouraged during the bad ones.

Despite 90% loss of kidney function, Frankie showed no noticeable signs of illness until four days before his death. (Photo by Kathy Smith)

Liver Disease

The early stages of liver disease have few visible symptoms, though some rabbits experience weight loss. Liver problems are usually detected by blood work for an unrelated (or undefined) problem. Abnormal values in one or more of the following tests may indicate liver problems:

- SGOT
- SGPT
- Total Bilirubin
- Alkaline Phosphatase

An enlarged liver may also be noticed on an x-ray, in which case your veterinarian will probably suggest blood work to help assess the extent of the problem. If x-rays and blood work suggest liver disease, your veterinarian may suggest an abdominal ultrasound and a liver biopsy.

The following treatments have been effective in improving the above lab values:

- Milk Thistle (available at health food stores)
- Lactulose (requires a prescription from your veterinarian)

Both help take ammonia from the blood and are a tonic for the liver. As always, consult your veterinarian before treating a rabbit with either of these products.

Note: Use of cedar or pine shavings as litter or bedding can lead to liver damage. Depending on the individual rabbit and the length of exposure, damage may be reversible or there may be residual permanent damage. If your rabbit has spent time on cedar or pine, it is wise to do blood work a month or so after the last exposure so baseline liver values will be available if problems arise in the future. If values are high, ask your veterinarian whether treatment with Milk Thistle and Lactulose might help.

The liver can also be attacked by one species of coccidia. If liver disease is suspected and a fecal exam shows the presence of coccidia, your veterinarian will probably prescribe a 10-day treatment with Albon® suspension.

Lauren (left) spent the first two years of her life on cedar bedding. Thankfully, she had no lasting ill-effects and has lived a healthy life with her mate of four years, Mr. McGregor. (Photo by Kathy Smith)

Heart Disease

Little has been written about heart disease in rabbits. It is thought that the sudden death of many outdoor hutch rabbits is the result of a heart attack brought on by fear of danger—either real or perceived. However, owners who keep their rabbits outdoors rarely have a necropsy (the veterinary equivalent of an autopsy) done.

With rabbits living to an older age and rabbit caretakers becoming more educated about various diseases and what to watch for, veterinarians across the country are beginning to see and treat more rabbits with heart disease. Today we are breaking new ground, but as more cases are treated, more will be learned and hopefully heart disease in rabbits will become as treatable as it has become in humans.

Types of Heart Disease

Heart disease, in humans as well as animals, is most often thought of as a disease of the elderly, something that happens when the heart simply begins to "wear out." However, it is important to remember that there are congenital heart problems resulting from improper development before birth. Heart disease can also be caused by infection (bacterial, viral, parasite, or fungal) which can strike at any age. If you notice the symptoms described in this section, consult your veterinarian immediately. Don't assume your rabbit is too young to have heart disease.

The following are some of the heart conditions veterinarians are already seeing and treating with some success:

- **Cardiomyopathy.** Any disease that affects the **myocardium** (muscle of the heart wall), usually resulting in an enlarged and less efficient heart.

- **Pulmonary Congestion.** Excessive accumulation of fluid in the lungs.

- **Congestive Heart Failure (CHF).** Abnormal condition that reflects impaired cardiac pumping caused by an MI, ischemic heart disease, or cardiomyopathy. Symptoms may include pulmonary congestion or peripheral edema (swelling).

- **Tachycardia.** Rapid heart beat.

- **Arrhythmia.** Irregular heart beat.

In a few cases, autopsies have identified heart attack or heart failure as a likely cause of death. Because rabbits are herbivores, they **may** be less likely than humans to suffer from some heart ailments such as high blood pressure and hardening of the arteries, which are thought to be partially related, in humans, to the amount of fat in our diets (especially meat and dairy products).

Symptoms

The first symptoms of heart disease that will be visible to a rabbit caretaker will probably be decreased activity, breathing difficulties and changes in eating habits (which may be a result of breathing difficulties). Initially, there may be subtle, almost unnoticeable, changes in habits that suggest breathing problems. These may include:

- **Changes in activity patterns.** A rabbit who usually tears through the house may run less or stop to rest more frequently.

- **Heavier than normal breathing (almost panting) after exercise.**

- **Panting for no apparent reason while resting.**

- **Changes in eating habits.** Sudden reluctance to eat food directly from the floor (or difficulty eating when the head is angled down) may be a sign that your rabbit is having trouble breathing when the head is in certain positions.

- **Sudden reluctance to lie flat.** If a rabbit who normally spends a lot of time in a flopped position (on stomach or side) suddenly appears to have trouble getting comfortable when lying flat, this may be a sign that he is having trouble breathing in this position.

- **Obvious difficulty breathing when held in certain positions (e.g., on his back).**

If you notice one or more of the above symptoms, ask your veterinarian to do a thorough exam to rule out heart problems.

Diagnosis

If your veterinarian suspects heart disease, she will probably suggest doing a chest x-ray as the first diagnostic step. An x-ray will show problems such as an enlarged heart and/or fluid in the chest cavity that may indicate heart disease.

In some cases, the first indication of possible heart disease may be seen in an x-ray taken to examine the GI system. Note that lung abnormalities don't always indicate heart disease. They can also result from other causes including but not limited to cancer, infections, or trauma. Your veterinarian will probably suggest additional tests—minimally a thorough physical examination and blood work, including electrolyte levels—to narrow the diagnosis.

If heart disease is strongly suspected, your veterinarian will probably suggest additional tests to help determine the type and extent of damage to the heart. These tests may include:

- **Electrocardiogram (ECG or EKG).** A record of the electrical activity generated by the heart muscles. A paper printout of the results is normally generated. An ECG is used to diagnose specific heart problems including arrhythmia.

- **Echocardiogram.** Graphic outline of the movements of the heart structures compiled from ultrasound vibrations echoed from the heart structures. The results of this test can be captured on videotape. An echocardiogram provides information on the size of the heart chambers, the thickness of the walls, and contractility, which are all indicators of how well the heart is actually functioning.

Note that both of the above tests are not frequently performed on rabbits, and the veterinarians who perform them may have no experience with rabbits. Before having these tests performed, make sure your veterinarian has located someone who can interpret the results **for a rabbit!** Since results of both tests can be captured in a permanent format, the person interpreting the results need not be local.

Treatments

Antibiotics. If your veterinarian suspects heart disease that is caused by a bacterial infection in the heart muscle or valves, she will probably start antibiotic therapy. Although you can't culture heart bacteria, your veterinarian may suggest a blood and/or urine culture. As with most bacterial infections, she may prescribe an antibiotic after taking a sample for culture/sensitivity but before the results are back. If the culture/sensitivity suggests a different antibiotic would be more effective, therapy can be changed. If the culture/sensitivity comes back negative, your veterinarian will decide whether to continue therapy based on how your rabbit is responding clinically. Recent experience also suggests that **persistent** infections elsewhere in the body, or their associated inflammation, might be releasing heart muscle irritants which can result in arrhythmias. Appropriate antibiotics appear effective in eliminating these arrhythmias.

Diuretics. If there appears to be excess fluid in the chest cavity, a diuretic such as Lasix® (furosemide) may be prescribed. Be aware that with a diuretic, your rabbit will urinate more frequently and more profusely—and he may not be as good about using the litter-box. Be patient with him and be prepared for extra cleanup. Depending on how severe the problem is, you may consider diapers and/or wee-wee pads to help keep your rabbit dry.

Fluids. If your rabbit is on a diuretic, it is important to ensure that sufficient fluids are being consumed (either orally or subcutaneously) to keep your rabbit from becoming dehydrated. Depending on the health of your rabbit's kidneys and any antibiotic therapy being used, your veterinarian may suggest subcutaneous fluids. It may take some time—and close monitoring by both you and your veterinarian—to find the right fluid/diuretic balance.

Oxygen. If your rabbit's breathing is particularly labored, your veterinarian may want to hospitalize your rabbit for a short period (usually one to three days) and place him in an oxygenated incubator. Normally, oxygen is required only until the diuretic has time to clear out excess fluids and the fluid/diuretic balance has been adjusted.

ACE Inhibitors are often the first type of heart medication a veterinarian will try when a rabbit is diagnosed with heart disease, especially cardiomyopathy and CHF. Ace inhibitors such as Enalapril relax the blood vessels, allowing more oxygen-rich blood to reach the heart and may also help prevent damage to the heart muscle. The most common side effect of this class of drug in humans is a dry cough. ACE Inhibitors can be given alone or in conjunction with a diuretic and/or beta blocker.

Most rabbits who have been treated with Enalapril have tolerated it well. However, when Murray was diagnosed with an enlarged heart and cardiomyopathy, we started him on the dose of Enalapril that Dr. Allan had used on other rabbits. Within a couple of hours of his first dose, Murray, who has shown sensitivity to other medications, specifically opiates, was extremely lethargic and "zoned out." Rather than discontinue the treatment, we lowered the dose and he is both tolerating and responding well to a dose that is half of the original dose.

Beta Blockers (also known as Class II Anti-arrhythmics) slow the nerve impulse to the heart, making it work less hard, and also block the impulses that can cause arrhythmia. **Selective** beta blockers such as Atenolol target only the beta-1 receptors which are responsible for heart rate and strength of heartbeat. The primary side-effects of beta-blockers are fatigue and cold extremities. Murray is able to tolerate a significantly higher total daily dose of Atenolol by giving a smaller amount twice a day rather than a higher once-a-day dose. Beta blockers can be given alone or in conjunction with an ACE Inhibitor and/or diuretic.

Calcium Channel Blockers (also know as Class IV Anti-arrhythmics) such as Diltiazem slow the rate at which calcium passes into the heart muscles and into the vessel walls, causing the vessels to relax.

CoQ10 is a vitamin-like substance whose actions resemble those of Vitamin E. It is a powerful antioxidant, which prevents the formation of free radicals which can damage cells, and plays a critical role in the body's ability to produce energy. CoQ10 aids circulation, lowers blood pressure, enhances immunity, and allows more oxygen to be carried to the cells. Research in humans has shown that CoQ10 has increased the function and strength of the heart muscle and improved dilation of the veins.

Vitamin E is an antioxidant which reduces blood pressure, strengthens capillary walls, and improves the usage of oxygen in the heart. When giving Vitamin E to your rabbit, be sure it is **natural** Vitamin E.

Garlic contains many sulfur compounds which it uses to heal. It lowers blood pressure, improves circulation, and lowers cholesterol, triglyceride, and fat levels in the blood. It is effective in preventing blood clots in the vascular system and reduces arthrosclerosis, which reduces the chance of stroke or heart attack.

Hawthorn is an herb that is often described as a "tonic for the heart." It has been effective in the treatment of chest pain, congestive heart failure (CHF), arrhythmia, and blood pressure (whether high or low). It increases coronary and myocardial blood flow by dilating and relaxing coronary blood vessels, thus increasing blood flow without increasing pressure. In addition, it has a mild diuretic effect. Its mechanism of action is believed to be similar to that of

Class III Anti-arrhythmics which slow electrical impulses in the heart by blocking the heart's potassium channels. Hawthorn may be given **cautiously** along with other medications described above. **Lower** doses of ACE inhibitors may be appropriate with hawthorn since hawthorn has similar effects. **Hypertension** has been reported when hawthorn has been used with some beta-blockers. According to the <u>PDR for Herbs</u>, **hawthorn should not be given with Propulsid®** (see the discussion of Hawthorn in the Herbal Remedies section for more detail). Also, be aware that, like other herbal remedies, the benefits of hawthorn may not be seen for a number of weeks; thus, the traditional heart medications may be necessary for initial treatment of life-threatening heart conditions.

Sasha (left) was diagnosed with heart arrhythmia and was treated with enalapril, giving her an extra 18 months with her loving family. Hazy (right) was diagnosed with a heart murmur and structural heart defects at age 5. Except for minor behavior changes, she functioned normally without medication for another two years before becoming extremely sensitive to heat. (Photo by Suzanne Trayhan)

Murray was diagnosed with cardiomyopathy at age 6 and with an arrhythmia three months later. He is being treated with enalapril, atenolol, Lasix®, and antibiotics. (Photo by Kathy Smith)

Cancer

There may be no more frightening diagnosis to hear for a friend or family member—human or animal—than cancer. Though there are veterinary oncologists in many major cities across the country, few have experience treating rabbits. The few documented cases of cancer treatment in rabbits have perhaps resulted in prolonging life, but not in curing the disease. However, if we assume that cancer in rabbits is a death sentence, no progress can be made in discovering viable treatments and, hopefully, some day a cure.

If your rabbit is diagnosed with cancer, you have three options:

- Fight the disease as aggressively as possible while preserving his quality of life. Even if you choose this option, you need to realize that your rabbit will probably ultimately die. However, aggressive treatment can buy you several precious months or even years with your friend and your efforts may help other rabbits in the future.
- Make the rabbit as comfortable as possible, without aggressive treatment, and euthanize when he can no longer be kept comfortable.
- Euthanize the rabbit immediately.

Some questions to consider before choosing the first option:

- **Does your rabbit want to live?** This is the most critical point to consider. If the prognosis is poor and, in your heart, you feel your rabbit is ready to go, it is probably selfish to try to keep him alive. However, even if the prognosis is poor, if you believe your rabbit wants to live, don't give up right away.

- **Do you have a skilled and trusted veterinarian who is devoted to helping your rabbit?** This is also a critical point. You obviously cannot do this alone. Your veterinarian need not have experience treating cancer in rabbits—or any other species. What she does need to have is a solid understanding of rabbit medicine, a willingness to consult with specialists to help identify and select treatment options, and an ability to work as part of a treatment team.

- **Do you have the resources to fight for your rabbit's life?** Fighting cancer is expensive. Caring for a critically ill rabbit requires tremendous physical and emotional energy. If you are unwilling or unable to devote a large portion of your life to your rabbit during the battle, perhaps it is best not to try. If family members are going to resent the amount of money, time, and energy this battle requires, you face a difficult choice. Remember, if you and your rabbit are going to fight the cancer, your rabbit needs to know he has your unconditional love and support.

What follows is the story of Smokey, a brave bunny who fought cancer for five months. Although the cancer ultimately won, those of us who fought with him did not fail. Smokey had five additional quality months with us—and taught us much about strength, courage, and unconditional love.

Smokey's Story

Smokey was a gray lop who entered our lives and stole our hearts in April 1994. His family was moving and decided not to take him—if we didn't want him, someone who raised rabbits for food would "dispose of" him. When he came to us he was four years old and had been severely neglected. He lived alone in an outdoor hutch. He had horrible malocclusion which no one had noticed. He cowered in the back of his cage and trembled when I held him. Within a month, however, he was chasing me around the back yard! It was such a joy to watch Smokey come out of his shell.

The following February, Smokey developed a stubborn ear infection. He bravely endured nine months of vet visits, antibiotic treatment, and ear flushes before finally being cured. He was a model patient—never fighting his medication and never acting sick. He and I really bonded during those nine months of medication—and Smokey became my first House Rabbit.

On December 4, 1997, Smokey was diagnosed with cancer. He had a huge mass in his mouth. I made it clear that money was not a consideration if there was hope for quality of life; however, I would **not** let him suffer. A year earlier we had watched my father-in-law die of prostate cancer. At the time I had said, "If he were a bunny, we wouldn't have to let him suffer like this." Dr. Bradley recommended we try surgery, and euthanize him if that seemed best once she got in there. Before the surgery, I kissed Smokey and told him how much I loved him and wanted him to get better. I also gave him permission to go peacefully.

Dr. Bradley removed as much of the tumor as she could but, sadly, she could not get it all. She was amazed at how well Smokey came through the surgery.

She wanted to keep him overnight, but agreed to let him come home. Later I was sure, in my heart, that he would not have survived if I had left him. He would have given up, thinking we had abandoned him. Smokey came home with Baytril® and Prednisone, which he was to be on for the rest of his life.

On the way to pick up Smokey I told my husband, George, "If he doesn't show an interest in food, we have to let him go." As soon as we got home, I opened his carrier. Before George could get into the house, Smokey had run—still wobbly from the anesthesia—to his pellets and tried to eat. Of course it was much too soon—roughly four hours after surgery. But it was a wonderful indication of how much he wanted to fight for his life. I set out a saucer of canned pumpkin (one of his favorite foods) and left him to rest.

A couple of hours later he came running—still a bit wobbly—out to the living room to be with his family. I spent much of the evening on the floor next to him and was rewarded with "bunny kisses." Throughout the evening I syringe fed small amounts of Gatorade to keep him hydrated. Dr. Bradley had told me that I could try syringe feeding canned pumpkin about bedtime. At 10:00 p.m. I sat on the floor next to Smokey with a fresh saucer of pumpkin. I put a small amount on my finger, stuck the finger in his mouth, and watched him eagerly eat the pumpkin. I continued feeding this way until he had eaten about a tablespoon. Twice during the night I got up and "hand-fed" more pumpkin.

The day after Smokey's surgery George and I took him back to learn how to give fluids. For Smokey, I overcame a lifelong fear of needles. The biopsy results came in later that day, confirming our worst fears. Smokey had a spindle cell carcinoma—very aggressive and fast-growing. After consulting with the local specialists, one of the country's top rabbit specialists, and a veterinary oncologist in California who had worked with rabbits before specializing in oncology, Dr. Bradley recommended chemotherapy with Doxorubicin, with treatments planned at four-week intervals. She was very open about the risks. The drug was known to have cardiotoxicity side-effects, and this effect was known to be cumulative. This meant that Smokey might die during the treatment itself—and that the risk increased with each subsequent treatment. By the fifth or sixth dose, death was likely. However, Dr. Bradley reminded me that if we did nothing he would almost certainly die—and probably soon. Smokey would be anesthetized for chemotherapy, so if death occurred, it would be painless.

The decision to try chemotherapy for Smokey was one of the hardest I have ever made. I'm not sure I would choose to endure chemotherapy myself—how could I even consider subjecting Smokey to it? But he made it clear he wanted to fight—so how could I choose to do nothing? A veterinary student I "met" via e-mail reassured me by explaining that the goals of chemotherapy in human and veterinary medicine were different: In human medicine the goal is to cure, often at the expense of quality of life, whereas in veterinary medicine the goal is to prolong quality life.

We scheduled Smokey's first treatment for December 12. During the week between surgery and chemotherapy, Smokey was quieter than before surgery but very sociable. He gained strength each day and his appetite was actually better than it had been in months. The night before chemotherapy, Smokey went back to our bedroom and played under the bed—something he hadn't done in months. Once again I wondered if I was doing the right thing.

Dr. Bradley met us at the specialists' office on December 12. She administered the anesthesia and monitored vital signs while the specialist administered the Doxorubicin. Before they took Smokey away I told him, as I had before surgery, that I knew he was brave and strong and could get through this, but that if he was ready to give up, this would be an easy way for him to go. The Doxorubicin had to be given very slowly, so it was almost an hour and a half before Smokey was back in my arms, giving me bunny kisses. I don't think I've ever been that scared. Dr. Bradley said he did **great** during the actual treatment but "crashed" coming out of the anesthesia. They got his temperature back up with makeshift hot water bottles made from rubber gloves. Dr. Bradley took him back to the clinic for observation for a few hours.

Smokey showed no ill-effects after chemotherapy. He was a bit quieter and his appetite was down slightly for the first couple of days, but he bounced back quickly. Ten days after chemotherapy—just before Christmas—we took him in for blood work to check for immune-system problems that would make additional chemotherapy inadvisable. The results were good and we scheduled his second chemotherapy for January 9.

By Christmas we had settled into a routine and I couldn't have asked for a better patient. Smokey took his medicines willingly. I had become comfortable giving fluids and Smokey often groomed himself during the process. George and I stayed home as much as possible and when we did go out, we left Smokey loose in the whole house with the TV on for company. Friends and family who visited us over the holidays were amazed at how good he looked. All of them said that you would never guess by looking at him that he was being treated for cancer.

Since Smokey's temperature had dropped sharply after the first treatment, I packed a bag for his January 9 treatment—soft towels, a hot water bottle covered with soft fabric (bunny-shaped, of course), and an instant heat pack. Dr. Bradley had a little more trouble finding a vein this time, but otherwise she felt the treatment had gone better than the first time. We got to bring Smokey home immediately. Dr. Bradley also felt certain that the mass had not grown any and had perhaps even gotten smaller.

Again, Smokey showed no serious side-effects from his chemotherapy. His appetite and energy levels were down slightly for the first few days, but returned quickly. Ten days later when we took Smokey in for blood work some of the immune-system values were down. We decided to wait five weeks for the next chemotherapy and do blood work again first.

On January 27 Smokey suddenly stopped eating. Dr. Bradley saw what looked like an abscess in the mouth along with some regrowth of the tumor. She put him on Septra® along with the Baytril®, had me give Banamine® shots twice a day, and told me to syringe feed as much as possible to put some weight on him. We scheduled surgery for Friday, January 30 to drain the abscess. As always, Smokey was a wonderful patient for those three days. He took the new medication willingly and actually enjoyed being syringe-fed several times a day.

When Dr. Bradley got into Smokey's mouth, she discovered that what had looked like an abscess was actually food that was caught on the tumor, which was much larger than the first time. This time, however, it had grown across the mouth instead of back into the throat, so she was able to remove more of it. She did blood work and sent a sample of the mass off for analysis, hoping this would tell us whether the chemotherapy was helping. We reminded each other that it had been eight weeks since his initial surgery—longer than either of us had dared to hope.

Results of the biopsy and blood work were not encouraging. There was no indication that the chemotherapy was helping and RBC values were continuing to fall. Dr. Bradley consulted with the local specialists again; they had just added a veterinary oncologist. There was another more expensive drug that we could try. Carboplatin would be safer because it did not have the cardiotoxic side-effects that Doxorubicin had. However, anorexia was a common side-effect. This concerned me because Smokey wasn't eating that well and was beginning to lose weight. However, Dr. Bradley reminded me that a rabbit's GI system is very different from humans, dogs, and cats—the species the drug had been used on.

We scheduled chemotherapy for February 20 to allow Smokey time to recover from surgery. At my suggestion, we began regular weekly checkups. We kept Smokey on all previous medications and added Pet-Tinic® Vitamins, a low dose of Rimadyl® to make him more comfortable, and Epogen® injections to help boost RBC. I continued to syringe-feed three times a day, cradling Smokey in my arms like I was feeding a baby.

Both doctors thought Smokey's first chemotherapy with Carboplatin went very smoothly. The procedure went much faster, as this drug did not have to be administered as slowly. Dr. Bradley said his color came back much faster than it had before and the oncologist said the treatment had gone as well as he had ever seen in any animal.

A week later, at Smokey's regular checkup, Dr. Bradley saw a small amount of regrowth of the cancer. It had been exactly four weeks since his last surgery and we both knew the new chemotherapy had not yet had time to work. We scheduled surgery for the following Tuesday, March 3, hoping that since we were catching the growth earlier this time the mass would be smaller and the surgery shorter. Because the surgery was less invasive, Smokey bounced back quickly. We continued with all medications and syringe feeding. On March 13 we did blood work again and scheduled chemotherapy for March 20. Again, the treatment went smoothly, with no noticeable side-effects.

Around the first of April, Smokey's appetite began to decrease and he was losing more weight. Dr. Bradley expressed concern about all the medications he was on, especially the combination of Rimadyl® and Prednisone. Reluctantly, I agreed to take him off the Rimadyl. More than anything, I didn't want Smokey to be in pain. Almost immediately, I felt that Smokey was uncomfortable. Dr. Bradley reluctantly put him back on the Rimadyl and discontinued the Septra®. I began to syringe-feed more frequently to keep Smokey's weight up. We had a wonderful Easter together. In December, I had simply prayed for Christmas together, never daring to hope he would make it to Easter!

We had tentatively scheduled chemotherapy for April 17. However, the Monday after Easter, when I was giving him medicine, I was sure I saw a mass, so I scheduled an extra checkup for Wednesday. Dr. Bradley looked at the part of the mouth where the mass had always been and saw nothing. But I insisted, holding him on his back, opening his mouth with a medicine dropper, and pointed out what I had seen. Sure enough, it was a fairly large mass that was positioned in front of where Dr. Bradley was looking with the otoscope. We cancelled the chemotherapy for the 17th and scheduled surgery instead.

Smokey's surgery was scheduled for 10:30 a.m. At 4:30 a.m. I syringe-fed him. Around 8:00 a.m. he ate most of 1/4 slice of bread and tried to eat some pellets for the first time since the beginning of April. I know he was telling me how very much he wanted to stay with us. However, Dr. Bradley was very discouraged after surgery. The mass was much larger than ever before. It went all the way across the roof of the mouth and back part way into the esophagus. She was amazed that he was even able to swallow when I syringe fed him—let alone eat the bread that morning! She clearly felt we were reaching the end of the road. She suggested that we either stop treatments completely or, if we continued, that we put him under anesthesia at least monthly so she could get a good look at the mouth.

Smokey never really bounced back from that surgery. However, he remained sociable and patiently endured the fluids and medicine he was given. Because of the weight he had lost, I syringe fed four to five times a day. He continued to accept that eagerly, ate bread on his own, and begged for his yogurt. Still, I knew things weren't OK.

George went with me to Smokey's April 24 checkup. Dr. Bradley immediately noticed that one side of Smokey's face was swollen and filled with fluid. She took several samples, using a needle, for analysis. This was the only time in almost five months of treatment that Smokey really flinched in pain during a procedure. It broke my heart. As gently as she could, Dr. Bradley let us know it was time to start thinking about saying goodbye. She put him back on Septra®, added Lasix® to help with the fluid buildup, and had me put warm compresses on his swollen face three times a day. We scheduled a follow-up appointment on April 29.

Throughout all this, Smokey remained somewhat active and extremely social, continuing to spend time wherever we were. By now he was eating almost nothing on his own, though he still eagerly accepted the syringe-feeding. Twice I carried a jar of his "gruel" into the living room to finish stirring while watching TV, then set the jar on the floor, waiting for a commercial before going back to the kitchen to fill the syringe. Both times Smokey went over to the jar and tried to eat from the jar—clearly letting me know he was ready to be fed.

Despite frequent syringe-feeding, Smokey had lost more weight by April 29. On May 1 Smokey had his final surgery. The mass was big again and this time there was evidence of abscessing. Dr. Bradley removed what she could. Either gum tissue or cancer had completely covered his lower molars, explaining why he could no longer chew even bread. I suggested x-rays. They showed abnormality in the jaw, indicating that the cancer was spreading there as well. We all knew we were at the end of the road. We would keep Smokey comfortable as long as possible, but knew we were now counting our time together in days.

I arranged to work at home most of the following week, knowing it would probably be our last week with Smokey. Tuesday evening, for the first time, I found myself really force-feeding the gruel. Smokey could really no longer swallow it—and nearly choked before I realized it was time to stop. After he recovered, I tried a little canned pumpkin, but even it was too solid. I decided that from that point on I would only feed baby food—and only when Smokey wanted it. The remainder of his life would be lived on his terms.

Wednesday Smokey eagerly ate the baby food and we had a wonderful evening with him. Thursday morning he still begged for food, but ate much less. He seemed to be having trouble breathing. I gave him Lasix, which helped a little. Around 1:00 I knew it was "time." I got a shallow box to set him on for support and lined it with soft towels. I set Smokey on the towels, but he refused to stay. He **ran** across the room and hopped on his favorite shelf. Even though it was clearly "time," Smokey was making it clear that he was still not ready to give up. I lifted him gently back onto the box and carried him to the car. On May 7, 1998, Smokey made a peaceful exit from this world as I held his head, stroked him, cried, and told him how much he was loved.

CARE OF THE CHRONICALLY ILL

This chapter discusses the challenges you will face when caring for a critically or chronically ill bunny. Whether you are dealing with an acute form of one of the "common" illnesses or a chronic problem, the challenges are the same. Even if you have no medical—or even first-aid—training, you will need to develop some fairly advanced nursing skills. Don't be afraid of learning these skills, even if you consider yourself squeamish. When you need to learn to do things for a loved one, it is easier than you think.

Making sure you have the resources—financial, physical, and emotional—to care for a critically ill rabbit is every bit as important as having the technical skills needed to provide that care. Providing intensive care is stressful. When your rabbit is seriously ill, it is important to take care of yourself. Remember, you'll be of little help to your rabbit if you are sick yourself. Remember also that rabbits are acutely sensitive to their caretakers' emotions. It is important for you to remain hopeful and to make sure your rabbit knows he has your unconditional love and support.

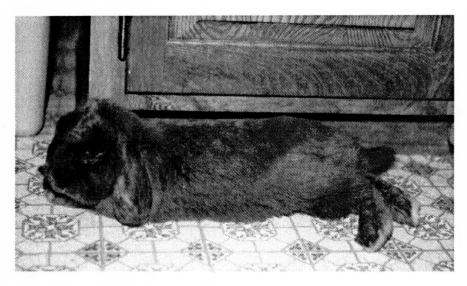

Smokey took over the kitchen during his nine month battle with chronic ear infections. (Photo by Kathy Smith)

Are You Willing to Pay the Price?

Caring for a critically ill rabbit will take its toll on you and those around you—financially, physically, and emotionally. It can also be a tremendously rewarding experience. As the primary caretaker of a critically ill bunny, you will develop an incredibly deep bond with him.

If you have a critically ill rabbit, the most important thing is to find a veterinarian you are comfortable trusting with your bunny's life. Hopefully, the section on *Being Prepared* motivated you to find this person before you needed her. Your veterinarian can help you assess whether your rabbit wants to fight and can give you an accurate picture of his prognosis. If the prognosis is poor and your rabbit has given up, euthanasia may, in fact, be the kindest answer for your rabbit. However, if the prognosis is good and/or your rabbit clearly wants to live, you may face a difficult decision: are you willing to pay the price to keep your rabbit alive?

Financial Costs

Financial costs are the easiest to recognize and assess. Before you face a crisis, think about how you would handle a serious medical emergency. If possible, start a "Rabbit Medical Fund" by saving a set amount each month in an account to be used only for rabbit health care. If you have a partner, discuss, in general terms, your willingness to sacrifice—perhaps even go into debt—to save your rabbit. This will give you an idea of how close—or far apart—your general philosophies are. Remember, however, that one or both attitudes **may** change drastically when faced with an actual crisis.

If your rabbit is diagnosed with a critical illness, have a frank discussion with your veterinarian about treatment options and costs. If you have financial limitations, discuss these openly. Ask if the clinic would consider a payment plan. Gather as much information as possible, then have a serious discussion with your partner and any other family members (including young children) who might have to make sacrifices. Try to get agreement from all that they are willing to make necessary sacrifices. If a partner or child resents making sacrifices and you decide to proceed with treatment, make sure to keep contact between that person and the ill rabbit to a minimum. Rabbits are extremely sensitive creatures who can sense negative feelings, which can affect your rabbit's will to live.

Physical Costs

Stress can have a tremendous impact on your physical health. Remember to take care of yourself—you can't help your bunny if you are sick yourself. If you have an established relationship with your family doctor, let him know that your treasured rabbit is seriously ill. If you don't already take a vitamin supplement, ask him to recommend one and take it faithfully. Try to continue to function without sleeping pills, sedatives, or antidepressants as these can cloud your thinking; however, if you have serious problems with insomnia or depression, don't hesitate to get the help you need. Remember also to eat well, get plenty of sleep, and exercise regularly.

Emotional Costs

Caring for a critically ill rabbit is emotionally draining. Expect a lot of ups and downs—your bunny will have good days and bad days. Remember to treasure every moment of those days when he feels good and try not to get too discouraged during the down times. Try to find something positive in each day—even if it is only that you had the day together.

Although you may want to spend every moment with your sick bunny, it is important to make time for friends and family who understand your love for your bunny and provide emotional support. If there is a local rescue group, they may be able to put you in touch with someone who has had a similar experience. If you don't know other rabbit people, you can find wonderful support from friends and co-workers who are true animal lovers who understand that you feel about your bunny the same way they feel about their dog or cat. Try to find at least two people—one at your workplace if at all possible—who will listen supportively. Talk openly about your fears and frustrations. Cry if it makes you feel better. By getting your emotions out in the open, it will be easier for you to maintain a positive attitude when you are at home caring for your ill rabbit.

The Internet is another excellent place to find both medical information and moral support. If you haven't already done so, this may be a good time to join one or more of the bunny e-mail lists (see the *Resources* section at the end of this book for more information). The people on these lists share your passion and dedication to your rabbit. If you reach out to them, they will provide understanding and encouragement. And someone who has nursed a rabbit through the same illness may have a suggestion that will make your rabbit more comfortable or even save his life!

Sadly, you will probably run into a lot of people who view rabbits as "disposable" pets and don't understand why you would want to spend the money on your bunny when you can "just get another one." Minimize contact with these people—you don't need the emotional stress they cause. If you get this reaction from close friends or family members, let them know in no uncertain terms that you need their support during this difficult time. If they can't do this for you, don't cut them off completely, but limit contact with them and avoid discussing your bunny.

Family and non-bunny friends shake their heads at the concept of weekly vet visits and regular acupuncture treatments. But Murray is worth every penny we have spent on him! (Photo by Kathy Smith)

Providing Intensive Care

The key to successful treatment and care of critically ill rabbits is in recognizing and reacting to the subtle changes that can occur very quickly in their health. Whether the care needed is simply extra love and attention, supportive care such as syringe-feeding, or an "advanced nursing procedure" such as giving sub-q fluids (fluids given under the skin via a needle) or injections, the first step is correctly identifying what is needed.

TLC

Perhaps the most important component of Intensive Care for a critically ill rabbit is spending time with him. The more time you spend, the more "in tune" you will be to subtle changes in his health or behavior.

Human attention is very important to a critically ill rabbit and can be a major factor in whether your rabbit chooses to give up or continue fighting. This is one reason I discourage hospitalizing a critically ill rabbit overnight unless someone is at the clinic 24 hours a day. A rabbit left alone at the clinic overnight may give up, thinking he has been abandoned. The same rabbit, returned to familiar surroundings with his human checking on him during the night, may decide to fight for his life.

Some critically ill rabbits (especially those who cannot care for themselves) do best if their human sleeps on the floor with them. Others do best sleeping alone but moving into their caretaker's bedroom. Still others will feel smothered by too much attention and actually prefer to have some quiet time to themselves in their own room. Let each individual rabbit's reactions to your attention guide you.

Some critically ill rabbits enjoy being held for long periods. This can be true for your rabbit, even if he normally hates to be held. Many caretakers report having held a rabbit that was near death through the night—often with reports of miraculous improvement by morning. Love may not be a scientific treatment for an illness, but it will go a long way in aiding recovery.

Supportive Care

If your rabbit cannot care for himself, there are a number of things you can do to make him more comfortable:

- If your rabbit is incontinent, paralyzed, or has difficulty using a litter-box, line his area with a synthetic sheepskin rug that allows urine to pass through but will keep the bunny dry. Have several of these on hand and wash them frequently.

- Encourage your rabbit to eat on his own by providing his favorite foods. Don't worry too much about what he eats—except for foods that pose an obvious threat to his life—the important thing is to keep him eating. Make sure fruits and vegetables are fresh and appealing. Try hand-feeding, providing love, sympathy, and encouragement with every bite. Turn eating into a social occasion—eat with your rabbit, sharing his food.

- Have fresh hay available at all times. If your rabbit prefers alfalfa to timothy, give him alfalfa. The important thing is to encourage him to eat.

- If your rabbit stops eating on his own, you will need to syringe-feed him. Many top rabbit veterinarians prescribe Oxbow's Critical Care; others believe pellet slurry made from your rabbit's usual brand of pellets is less likely to cause GI upsets. Other foods that may be syringe fed (with your veterinarian's approval) include canned pumpkin (100% pumpkin only, not pumpkin pie filling) or one of many recipes available that combine powdered pellets, baby food (watch for added sugar and onions and avoid these), pureed vegetables or fruit, and/or canned pumpkin. Be creative—try to incorporate one or more of your bunny's favorite foods, whether directly or through baby food. The primary goal is to keep the gut moving. Feed him as frequently as possible throughout the day, and as much as you can get down him at each feeding. When he clenches his teeth and won't swallow, stop for a while and try again later.

- If your rabbit needs help keeping clean, use a washcloth dampened with **warm** water and rub gently. This cleaning technique feels most like the bunny's natural way of grooming.

- Companionship is important. If your rabbit has a bonded mate, discuss the pros and cons of keeping them together with your veterinarian.

Unless they have started to fight, the stress (to both the sick and the well bunny) is probably of more concern than the danger of infection. Remember, the mate has already been exposed to the illness.

Occasionally you may need to separate a rabbit from his companions to allow healing from major surgery or to closely monitor food intake and fecal output. If you do need to isolate a member of a group temporarily, try to find a way to do so without completely separating them. Be resourceful! When I brought Goldie home after emergency GI surgery, I had to confine her. Goldie and her companions lived in my kitchen and dining room. In the pet store where I buy litter, I saw a puppy-training cage that looked just the right size to fit **under** my dining room table. It was a perfect fit, with a solid bottom to protect the carpet. While Goldie was confined I fed her companions their salad in the dining room next to Goldie's cage so they would encourage her to eat. After that, of course, the group always expected to be fed in the dining room and they had a litter-box there as well. Not exactly Martha Stewart, but this was a small price to pay for the joy of watching Goldie run and play as if she had never been at death's door.

If you have to completely separate the sick bunny from his mate, or if he is a "single" bunny, consider sleeping on the floor with him or at least moving him into your bedroom so he will not be alone at night.

Advanced Nursing Procedures

All rabbit caretakers need to learn how to give oral medications to their rabbit and how to take a rabbit's temperature. If you have a critically ill rabbit, you should also **have your veterinarian instruct you** in the following advanced nursing procedures:

•   **Sub-Q Fluids.** A critically ill rabbit will often require sub-q fluids (Lactated Ringers Solution or saline, depending on your rabbit's calcium levels). Your veterinarian may prescribe fluids daily or on an as-needed basis. Fluids help keep your rabbit hydrated, help with bouts of GI stasis, and keep electrolytes in balance. The fluids are the same as those given to humans through an IV and are available only through a veterinarian. They are administered as a "drip" via a large needle (usually 18 or 20 gauge) that is inserted under the skin along your rabbit's back. While some people prefer the 20 gauge needle because it is smaller, I prefer the 18 gauge because the fluids are administered faster, reducing the stress on both human and rabbit. **Note:** If you use the 18 gauge needle, pinch off the needle entry site for about 30 seconds after administering fluids and expect more seepage from the injection site since the larger needle creates a larger hole.

- **Injections.** When a rabbit is critically ill, chances are good that his caretaker, at some time, may need to give him injections. Some antibiotics are available only in injectable form. Others, like penicillin, are safe for rabbits only when given by injection. Often a timely injection of pain medication can jump-start a bunny's appetite, literally saving his life.

  Injections can be given either sub-q (under the skin) or intramuscularly. Sub-q injections are easier for a novice. Some medications can be deadly if injected into a vein. Make sure you completely understand the proper way to give a particular medication by injection.

Many people with no medical training—especially those with a real fear of needles—believe they could never learn to give fluids or injections. But when a special bunny is fighting for his life and needs this type of care, even the most squeamish of us can find the strength to do what we have to do for them. Remember, love will find a way.

After Goldie recovered from GI surgery, the Trio continued to enjoy eating their salad in our dining room. (Photo by Kathy Smith)

DIAGNOSIS AND CONVENTIONAL TREATMENTS

Successfully conquering illness is a two-step process. In cases of life-threatening illness, it is often necessary to begin treatment before results of all diagnostic tests are in. However, be wary of a doctor—whether animal or human—who routinely prescribes treatments without performing **any** diagnostic tests. Depending on the condition, culture/sensitivity tests, blood work, urinalysis, x-rays, or ultrasound may be helpful in pinpointing the problem. Never be afraid to ask your veterinarian if additional diagnostic procedures would be helpful.

Blood panels can be helpful in diagnosing a wide variety of problems. Unless you have medical training, when your veterinarian calls to discuss the results, you may feel "clueless" as to what your veterinarian is saying when she discusses the results. By understanding what the individual tests are for and what results are normally looked at together for diagnosing specific problems, you will be able to better understand your bunny's problem and ask intelligent questions. Don't be afraid to research medical conditions and their treatments on your own. It will help you understand the condition better and you might have more time to devote to researching treatments than your veterinarian.

When we think of conventional "western medicine" treatments, the first thing that comes to our mind is a prescription. In fact, we may feel short-changed if we pay for a veterinary (or human doctor) visit and don't come away with prescription drugs. It is important to know that **there is no such thing as a completely safe drug** and almost no drugs have been formally tested for use in rabbits. The section on drugs discusses the various classes of drugs that have been used on rabbits with **relative** safety and the drugs that you should **never** give your rabbit. The drug section discusses the conditions for which these drugs are normally prescribed, common "brand names," and precautions including length of use, common side-effects, and known drug interactions. Dosing information is not included in this book since it is important to always consult a veterinarian if your rabbit is ill.

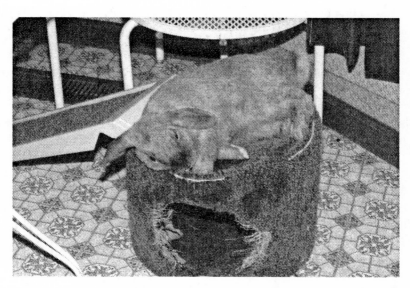

A cat condo with ramp provides Murray with both a place to exercise and a place to relax between trips to the vet. (Photo by Kathy Smith)

Diagnostics

While it is true that medicine is not an exact science, medical tests can take a lot of the guesswork out of diagnosis and treatment. Some veterinarians hesitate to suggest diagnostic tests for rabbits because most of their clients are unwilling to pay for these tests. It is up to you to make it clear that you recognize the value of diagnostic tests and are willing to pay for them.

Depending on clinical symptoms, diagnostic tests may be used either to confirm a diagnosis or to eliminate possibilities. While these tests often seem expensive, they may be critical to ensure proper treatment. Without test results to confirm (or eliminate) a diagnosis, your veterinarian must use the trial-and-error treatment approach. This can result in expensive and/or stressful treatments that are ineffective and sometimes actually harmful. For example:

- Treating a bacterial infection with an antibiotic to which the bacteria is resistant subjects your rabbit to the stress of being medicated and the potential side-effects of the antibiotic while having no positive impact on the disease.

- Treating head-tilt caused by *E. cuniculi* as if it were a bacterial ear infection (or vice-versa) allows a treatable, but potentially deadly, disease to continue to progress untreated. Both symptomatic *E. cuniculi* and severe bacterial infections need prompt treatment.

- Treating a yeast infection with antibiotics will only make the yeast infection worse. Yeast overgrowth is frequently a side-effect of antibiotic treatment because the antibiotic kills off the bacteria which keep yeast controlled.

While some diagnostic procedures may be difficult to arrange for your rabbit, most veterinarians can do the following tests:

- Cytology
- Culture and Sensitivity
- X-rays
- Urinalysis
- Blood Work

EKG's and ultrasounds are becoming more readily available, especially in larger metropolitan areas. CT-scans and MRI's, where available, are cutting edge diagnostic tools that can definitely aid in disease diagnosis.

You should never hesitate to ask your veterinarian if diagnostic tests would be useful in diagnosing and treating your rabbit's illness. Your question may prompt her to suggest one or more tests—or she may explain why she considers them unnecessary at this time.

Finally, if your rabbit has a serious condition and you are able to arrange for a specialized test (e.g., ultrasound or EKG), make sure you also have access to someone who can properly interpret the results **for a rabbit**. Don't assume your veterinarian has been trained to interpret tests done by specialists and don't assume the specialist has treated many rabbits. Options include having your veterinarian work closely with the specialist to interpret the test results or having her consult with one of the country's rabbit specialists.

Cytology

Cytology involves taking a sample from the infected area, staining it, and examining it under a microscope. A good veterinarian can quickly determine whether bacteria, yeast, or both are present in the sample and prescribe appropriate treatment. However, when bacteria are present, especially with chronic infections, a culture and sensitivity is advised to confirm that the most effective drug is being used. Cytology can also be used to give further information on soft tissue masses via a fine needle aspirate. Depending of the cell type(s) present and their characteristics, further information on an underlying inflammatory lesion, infection, or tumor can be gained.

Culture and Sensitivity

Culture and sensitivity testing involves taking a sample from the infected area, allowing bacteria to grow in a laboratory, and then testing a variety of antibiotics to identify drugs that are effective (and ineffective) against it. For best results, culture and sensitivity should be done prior to any treatment, especially with antibiotics.

Culture and sensitivity tests sometimes need to be repeated during the course of antibiotic treatment. For best results, your rabbit should be off medication for a minimum of three and preferably seven days before the follow-up culture/sensitivity is done. However, if your veterinarian does not feel antibiotics can be stopped without risk to your rabbit's health, a follow-up culture/sensitivity test can still be useful. If there is no growth, current antibiotic therapy is probably effective and should be continued until symptoms have been absent for some time (to be defined by your veterinarian). If, however, bacteria grow, your rabbit has either developed a secondary infection or the original bacteria have become resistant to the drug currently being used. Your veterinarian will decide whether to change antibiotics or add a second drug to treat the new or resistant infection.

X-rays and Ultrasound

X-rays can be useful as a general diagnostic tool, allowing your veterinarian to see the relative size, position, and condition of critical organs. They can show the presence of skeletal problems such as spondylosis as well as tumors and abscesses that might otherwise go undetected. Although the body is most frequently x-rayed, head x-rays, when properly taken and interpreted, can provide valuable information about dental problems and some upper respiratory and ear infections.

In most cases, your veterinarian will want to x-ray a rabbit experiencing GI stasis to ensure there is no blockage before treating with GI motility drugs such as Reglan® or Propulsid®. Use of these drugs when there is a blockage **can** cause the stomach or gastrointestinal tract (GIT) to rupture. X-rays can also show the amount of fluid or gas in the GI system, which can help your veterinarian develop the most appropriate treatment plan.

If x-rays show abnormality in a vital organ such as liver, kidney, or heart, your veterinarian may suggest an ultrasound to further diagnose the problem. While an ultrasound is significantly more expensive than an x-ray, it is a valuable diagnostic tool. In addition to providing more information on vital organs, ultrasound can often be used to rule out tumors and other serious problems. The cost of this test may be a small price to pay for "peace of mind."

Urinalysis

Urinalysis is useful in diagnosing a variety of urinary tract problems. The presence of bacteria in the urine indicates some form of urinary tract infection. Your veterinarian will probably want to do a culture/sensitivity test to identify the bacteria and determine appropriate antibiotic therapy. High calcium levels may confirm a diagnosis of bladder sludge. If high urine calcium levels are discovered before other symptoms of sludge appear, simple diet changes may stop sludge development in its early stages. Urinalysis can also be useful in diagnosing kidney failure.

Blood Tests

Blood panels are among the most useful diagnostic tools available to your veterinarian—and among the most confusing to the layman. Your veterinarian will interpret your rabbit's blood test results in the context of his overall health, clinical signs, and medical history (including any medications he is on) as well as her experience with the laboratory her clinic uses. The information in this section is not intended to substitute for **or** cause you to question this interpretation by your veterinarian. Instead, it is my hope that this section will provide a framework to help the reader better understand your veterinarian's interpretation and help you ask better questions, allowing you to play a more active and informed role in your rabbit's health care decisions.

Blood work can provide important clues about a rabbit's general health or it can be used to check for specific diseases. The four tests that are looked at most closely when diagnosing liver problems are:

- SGPT
- SGOT
- Total Bilirubin
- Alkaline Phosphatase

Additional tests that are considered are LDH, total protein, and albumin.

The primary tests that are looked at when diagnosing kidney disease are:

- Red Blood Cell Count (RBC)
- Creatinine
- Blood Urea Nitrogen (BUN)

Additional tests that are considered include electrolytes (sodium, potassium, chloride), calcium, and phosphorus.

Some blood tests, specifically tests for *E. cuniculi* and pasteurella, are done only at specific laboratories in the country. These **specialty** laboratories are listed in the *Resources* section at the end of this book.

Standard lab results are usually broken down into **Hematology** (counts and analysis of red and white blood cells and platelets) and **Serum Chemistry** (presence of certain elements or enzymes in the blood). These tests are normally done at a central laboratory chosen by your veterinarian's office. Most laboratory test results include a numeric result for the test, the normal range of values for the test, and some flag indicating results that fall outside the normal range. Normal ranges for tests vary from species to species and often vary slightly from lab to lab. It is important that the ranges provided to your veterinarian by the lab are ranges for **rabbits**. They may vary slightly from the values given in this section, but if they are drastically different you should have your veterinarian confirm (1) that the laboratory **has** normal ranges for rabbits and (2) that the ranges for rabbits were used in analyzing your rabbit's test results.

Note: In rabbits, many lab values can be affected by the stress, including travel to the vet, handling by strangers, and the process of collecting the blood sample. Drastically out-of-range values may also result from improper processing of the sample or laboratory error. Your veterinarian will probably want to repeat any tests where results are significantly outside the normal range. Many veterinarians can run individual lab tests in their office, giving them almost immediate results.

Blood work is normally suggested by your veterinarian when your bunny is ill. However, if your rabbit has reached the age of five years without ever having blood work done, talk to your veterinarian about having a baseline blood panel done. In many diseases, **change** in lab values is at least as important as the actual result. A slightly above (or below) normal value that has remained stable over a period of months or years may be of little concern to your veterinarian. However a drastic increase (or decrease) between two sets of tests may raise a red flag even though both values fall within the normal range.

Hematology

Hematology data consists of those tests that are part of a CBC (complete blood count). A CBC gives a complete picture of red and white blood cells (both quantity and composition) and platelets. CBC results may provide diagnostic information or may point to additional testing that is needed.

The principle function of red blood cells (erythrocytes) is to transport oxygen through the body. CBC components related to **red blood cells** include:

- Red Blood Cell (RBC) Count
- Hemoglobin (Hgb) is a complex protein-iron compound in red blood cells that carries oxygen to the cells from the lungs and carbon dioxide away from the cells to the lungs.
- Hematocrit (HCT) is a measure of the packed cell volume of red cells expressed as a percentage of the total blood volume
- Mean Corpuscular Hemoglobin (MCH) is the ratio of hemoglobin to RBC
- Mean Corpuscular Hemoglobin Concentration (MCHC) is the ratio of hemoglobin to hematocrit
- Mean Corpuscular Volume (MCV) is the average volume of each red cell derived from ratio of hematocrit to RBC

Below-normal RBC values normally point toward some form of anemia and/or blood loss. A decreased Packed Cell Volume (PCV) can help confirm the diagnosis of anemia. The relationships between hematocrit, hemoglobin, and total RBC can help to determine the type and severity of the anemia.

Decreased RBC may be caused by:

- a bone marrow disorder
- external blood loss from a wound or surgery
- internal hemorrhaging
- chronic liver or kidney disease
- anemia of chronic disease

Note: High doses of Ivermectin® can cause lowered RBC, hemoglobin concentration, hematocrit, mean corpuscular hemoglobin concentration, and mean corpuscular hemoglobin.

Polycythemia is defined by an increase in PCV, hemoglobin concentration, or RBC count. It may indicate critical heart or lung problems and may produce neurological symptoms such as seizures.

The primary function of white blood cells (leukocytes) is to resist and fight infection. **White blood cell** values are used to detect infection and/or inflammation.

The White Blood Cell (WBC) Count, along with the differentials described below, can indicate the amount and type of infection/inflammation present in the body.

Differential white blood cell counts can be used to evaluate a body's ability to resist or overcome infection/inflammation or to assess the stage, severity, and/or cause of the infection/inflammation. To properly interpret the differentials, the diagnostician must consider both the absolute values and their percent relative to total WBC.

The five components of differential white cell counts are:

1.   **Neutrophils** serve as the body's primary defense against bacteria, removing bacteria and debris. During inflammatory disease, neutrophils may collect as visible pus. Elevated neutrophil values may indicate inflammation or they may be the result of stress and/or fear or use of steroids.

2.   **Eosinophils** are involved in allergic responses and destruction of parasites. Elevated eosinophil values may be a sign of an allergic reaction or of parasites that have invaded the rabbit's tissues. In rabbits, eosinophils are also important in wound healing. Lowered eosinophil values are often the result of stress or use of steroids.

3.   **Basophils** aid eosinophils in fighting parasites.

4.   **Lymphocytes** initiate immune responses. Persistent, elevated lymphocyte values may be a sign of chronic infection or immune-mediated disease. Lowered lymphocyte values occur with some viral diseases or they may be the result of stress or use of steroids.

5.   **Monocytes** remove dead and injured cells, cell fragments, and microorganisms. Elevated monocyte values may indicate chronic infection or they may be the result of stress or steroid therapy.

Platelets, the smallest of the blood components, play a role in blood coagulation.

Serum Chemistry

SGOT (AST) is an enzyme found primarily in the cells of the liver, heart, skeletal muscles, and red blood cells. Elevated levels may indicate heart, liver, or muscular disease or hemolysis (spontaneous or artifactual). Stress, restraint procedures, and/or intramuscular injections can also cause elevated SGOT levels. Lowered SGOT levels are not considered significant.

Note: Many drugs including sulfonamides (e.g. Septra®) and glucocorticoids (e.g. Prednisone) can cause elevated SGOT levels.

SGPT (ALT) is an enzyme necessary for tissue energy production. It primarily appears in the liver, with lesser amounts in the kidneys, heart, and skeletal muscles. Elevated SGPT levels are nearly always an indicator of liver disease. However, the magnitude of the elevation does **not** correlate with the seriousness of the liver disease, nor is it indicative of the prognosis. Elevated SGPT may be the first detectable sign of liver disease and should be periodically monitored if other explanations for the elevation are not found.

Note: Many drugs including tetracyclines, glucocorticoids, and narcotic analgesics can cause falsely elevated SGPT levels. In rabbits, prolonged anesthesia can also elevate SGPT.

Bilirubin values (direct, indirect, and total) are used to evaluate the liver. Elevated bilirubin values nearly always indicate some degree of liver damage/disease or cholestasis (an interruption to the normal flow of bile). In cholestasis, both total and direct bilirubin will be elevated.

Alkaline Phosphatase can be used to detect liver and skeletal diseases. Elevated alkaline phosphatase levels, in conjunction with elevated levels of SGPT, SGOT, and/or Bilirubin, help confirm a diagnosis of liver disease or damage. Bone disease may also cause a mild elevation in alkaline phosphatase.

Note: Alkaline phosphatase levels fluctuate according to a rabbit's age, breed, and strain (but not by gender or time of day). Values are normally higher in young rabbits.

Blood Urea Nitrogen (BUN) is the chief end product of protein metabolism. It is formed in the liver from ammonia and excreted by the kidneys. Below-normal values may indicate severe liver damage or decreased dietary protein intake. Above-normal values usually indicate kidney disease, including tumors and renal failure. Kidney problems often show up in BUN levels before creatinine levels. However, renal failure will not show up in BUN levels until 50%–75% of renal function has been lost.

Note: There is a daily variation in BUN levels with peak values occurring between 4:00 p.m. and 8:00 p.m. Corticosteroid, aminoglycocide, or tetracycline therapy may elevate BUN levels. Anabolic steroids may lower BUN levels. Chloramphenicol therapy can falsely elevate or depress BUN levels, depending on the method of analysis used.

Creatinine is a waste product of the body's metabolism and is excreted in the urine. If the kidneys are not working properly, creatinine stays in the blood. Kidney damage/disease or severe muscle damage account for elevated creatinine levels. Creatinine levels are not altered by as many non-renal factors as BUN. As with BUN, renal failure will not show up in elevated creatinine levels until 50%–75% of renal function has been lost.

In rabbits, serum **calcium** levels are proportional to dietary calcium levels. Above normal calcium levels may indicate a diet that is too high in calcium. Elevated calcium levels may also be an indicator of cancer. Decreased serum calcium often occurs with diarrhea.

Phosphorus levels are regulated by the kidneys. In rabbits, decreased phosphorus levels often accompany an increase in urinary calcium excretion.

Potassium levels can be another indicator of kidney function. Elevated potassium levels may indicate renal failure or other kidney disease. Decreased potassium levels may accompany hypothermia, diarrhea, or polyuria (excessive urination).

Note: Nonsteroidal anti-inflammatory drugs (NSAIDS) may cause elevated potassium levels. High doses of IV penicillins, outdated tetracyclines, aminoglycocides, corticosteroids, diuretics, and aspirin may cause decreased serum potassium levels.

Sodium levels can be used to evaluate kidney function as well as fluid-electrolyte and acid-base balance. Elevated sodium levels may accompany hyperthermia, dehydration, or may be a residual effect of a prior episode of dehydration. Decreased sodium levels are often the result of diarrhea or polyuria (excessive urination). Persistent below-normal sodium levels may also indicate kidney, liver, or heart problems.

Note: Corticosteroid therapy may increase sodium levels. Nonsteroidal anti-inflammatory drugs (NSAIDS) and diuretics may decrease sodium levels.

Abnormal **chloride** levels are caused by the same diseases that affect sodium levels. High chloride levels may be the result of severe dehydration. Low chloride levels may result from diarrhea or polyuria (excessive urination).

Note: Diuretics may decrease chloride levels.

Elevated **total protein** levels may accompany dehydration, shock, or hyperthermia. Decreased total protein levels often occur with kidney or liver disease.

Note: Anabolic steroids and corticosteroid therapy many increase total protein levels.

In rabbits, albumin represents about 60% of total protein in contrast to 35%–50% in other mammals. Decreased **albumin** levels may indicate liver or kidney disease. Albumin is also usually lower in pregnant rabbits. The globulin portion of total protein (sometimes reflected only in the **Albumin/Globulin or AG Ratio**) may increase in cases of hypothermia.

Cholesterol levels are directly influenced by the thyroid, liver, and steroid producing organs. In rabbits, these values vary with age, breed, strain, sex, and time of day. Adult females generally have higher cholesterol levels than adult males and peak values occur between 4:00 p.m. and 8:00 p.m. Elevated cholesterol levels are linked to the development of aortic atherosclerosis.

Lactic dehydrogenase (LDH) is present in most body tissues. Decreased LDH levels are not considered significant. Elevated LDH levels are not uncommon and, if no other abnormal lab values are found, are usually not significant. Rabbits with liver disease may have elevated LDH levels along with elevated values of SGOT, SGPT, and alkaline phosphatase. Occasionally, LDH levels will be more than three times normal in rabbits with malignancies.

Creatine phosphokinase (CPK) results are sometimes included in lab results and will probably be abnormally high. This test has little meaning for rabbits. Recent surgery or even the physical trauma of having blood drawn may be enough to cause very high CPK values.

In humans, abnormally high **serum glucose** levels are almost always associated with diabetes. There are two reasons that glucose levels are frequently very high in rabbits:

1.   Accurate glucose testing requires a fasting blood sample. Because of their sensitive GI systems, rabbits should never be fasted prior to any medical procedure. Therefore results are often elevated.

2.   Glucose levels in rabbits can be greatly increased by the stress associated with having blood drawn.

Diabetes is rare, but not unknown, in rabbits. Other symptoms of diabetes include:

•   Drinking excessively
•   Urinating more than usual
•   Frequent bacterial infections (because a diabetic's white cells don't function as well)

If your rabbit has one or more of the above symptoms along with extremely high glucose values (above 400), your veterinarian may ask for a urine sample to check urine glucose levels to help rule out diabetes.

Thyroid problems have not been frequently diagnosed in rabbits and the blood tests that detect thyroid disease are not part of standard blood work. In fact, we had difficulty finding a lab that had ever run a thyroid test on a rabbit when we began to suspect that Murray was suffering from hypothyroidism. Murray's initial symptoms included lethargy and weight gain accompanied by a **decreased** appetite. When his fur became coarse and unhealthy looking, we began to seriously suspect hypothyroidism. Thanks to the internet, we found someone in Canada whose rabbit had been diagnosed with hypothyroidism and we sent a blood sample to the lab she had used. Contact information on this lab is included in the *Resources* section at the end of this book. The lab confirmed that Murray's T3 levels were low. His symptoms improved after two months of treatment with Soloxine and subsequent T3 levels have been within the normal range.

Fred and Henrietta enjoy spending time cuddling and grooming each other. (Photo by Kathy Smith)

Lab Normal Ranges for Rabbits

As stated earlier in this section, normal ranges for lab tests vary from species to species and from lab to lab. This table on the next page contains broader ranges than are usually found on an actual lab report. It was created by comparing the values in the <u>Handbook of Rodent and Rabbit Medicine</u> by Laber-Laird, Swindle, and Flecknell with those from a lab report on one of my rabbits and creating a composite range using the lower of the two low values and the higher of the two high values. If your rabbit's blood results show many values that are flagged as out-of-range but fall within the ranges shown in this table, you may want to ask your veterinarian to confirm that the lab used the normal ranges for rabbits.

Test Name	Test Units	Normal Range
Hematology		
RBC	X 10^6/mm^3	3.8–8.0
PCV	%	30–50
Hemoglobin	g/dl	9.4–17.4
WBC	X 10^3/mm^3	2.6–12.5
Neutrophils %	%	12–55
Eosinophils %	%	0–3.4
Basophils %	%	0–6
Lymphocytes %	%	28–85
Absolute Lymphocyte	/UL	1500–7000
Monocytes %	%	0–13
Absolute Monocytes	/UL	0–850
Platelets	X 10^3/mm^3	270–480
MCV	FL	65–75
MCH	PG	12.5–17.5
MCHC	%	32–36
Serum Chemistry		
SGOT (AST)	IU/L	10–120
SGPT (ALT)	IU/L	10–80
Total Bilirubin	mg/dl	0–1.0
Alkaline Phosphatase	IU/I	4–20
Blood Urea Nitrogen	mg/dl	10–33
Creatinine	mg/dl	0.5–2.6
Calcium	mg/dl	5.5–15.5
Phosphorus	mg/dl	4.0–7.2
Potassium	mEq/l	3.7–10
Sodium	mEq/l	130–160
Chloride	mEq/l	90–120
Total Protein	g/dl	5.4–8.3
Albumin	g/dl	2.4–4.6
Globulin	g/dl	2.9–4.9
Cholesterol	mg/dl	10–80
LDH	IU/I	34–129
Glucose	mg/dl	78–155

Test Name	Test Units	Normal Range
Miscellaneous Normal Values		
Blood Volume	ml/kg	49–59
Urine Volume	ml/24hrs	20–350
Urine Ph		7.6–8.8
Heart Rate	/min	120–325
Respiration Rate	/min	30–60

Drugs

While drug therapy (both prescription and non-prescription) is the most common treatment for most illnesses, it is important to understand both the benefits and the risks. This is especially important for bunnies. There are a number of things that every rabbit caretaker should understand about drug therapy:

1.   Most drugs have not been specifically tested and approved for use in rabbits. Therefore, there is much less information available about the effects—good and bad—of most drugs on rabbits, and very little of this is available from the manufacturers. Both safety and efficacy information for rabbits comes primarily from information shared among veterinarians and from experiences of rescuers and individual rabbit caretakers.

2.   While some classes of drugs are safer for rabbits than others, no drug should be considered totally safe. All drugs have potential side-effects and not all rabbits react the same way to the same drug. Any time your rabbit is on medication of any type, you should watch carefully for changes in behavior and consult your veterinarian at the first sign of abnormal behavior.

3.   If you work with more than one veterinarian, **always** make sure the doctor you are seeing is aware of **all** medications (prescription, over-the-counter, and herbal) your rabbit has been exposed to and all procedures he has undergone within the prior four weeks. Some drugs, including anesthetics, have residual effects that can interact with other medications long after they were used. Some drug interactions can be deadly, so make sure your veterinarian has your rabbit's complete recent medical history.

4.   A rabbit's GI system is very different from that of a cat or dog. Medications (such as oral penicillin) that may be appropriate for other species can be deadly to rabbits. Similarly, some medications (such as Banamine®) that cause problems in other species are excellent bunny drugs. Thus, it is critical to work with a veterinarian who is experienced with rabbits.

This section will address the most commonly prescribed classes of medications:

- Antibiotics/Antifungals (both systemic and topical)
- Analgesics (Pain Relievers)
- Steroids
- GI Medications

Dosing

Dosage information is not included in this book because it is critical that drugs, both prescription and over-the-counter (OTC), be given only under the supervision of a qualified rabbit veterinarian. Appropriate doses for **most** drugs are given **by the manufacturer** as a range based on body weight. Your veterinarian may prescribe at the low end of the dose range and increase the dose if your rabbit's condition does not improve; or she may prescribe at the high end of the range and decrease the dose if side effects occur. Both approaches are valid. Your veterinarian's decision will be based on the severity of the condition being treated, her experience with the particular drug and its side effects, and your rabbit's medical history (including other medications and general tolerance for drugs). You may want to ask your veterinarian whether she is giving a high or low dose of the drug, particularly if you plan to discuss your rabbit's illness and treatment with other rabbit parents. This information will also help you know whether to be more watchful for side-effects or lack of improvement in your rabbit's condition. **Never** change the dose of your rabbit's medication without first discussing the change with your veterinarian.

Drug Safety Factors

It is hard to work for 20+years in the pharmaceutical industry (working with data from clinical trials) without developing a very cautious perspective on the factors that define drug safety: side effects, interactions, and a patient's medical history. Be very wary of **anyone** who claims a medication is "completely safe." I have chosen to err on the side of caution and list as **warnings** those side effects and interactions that have actually been observed in rabbits **and** those that can be life-threatening, **even if they have never been observed in a rabbit.** It is not unusual for rare but deadly side-effects to occur in one out of 500 or one out of 1000 patients. Indeed, there may be situations where, based on your rabbit's condition and the treatments already tried, your veterinarian may recommend a treatment or combination of treatments that include such a warning. If this happens, you and your veterinarian should openly discuss both the potential risks and the potential benefits of proposed treatment, and then make an **informed** decision whether to proceed.

When your veterinarian prescribes a drug, she will probably tell you about any "common" side effects. If she does not, ask if there is anything in particular you should watch for. The most common **easily observed** side-effects of many drugs are diarrhea/constipation and lethargy/hyperactivity—and yes, many drugs can cause completely opposite reactions in different patients. Other common side effects are more difficult to pinpoint in rabbits. If you sense your rabbit is "off" or simply "not feeling well", he **may** be suffering from nausea, depression, or another side effect from his medication. Finally, some medications can cause damage to the liver, kidneys, or other vital organs, especially when used long-term. This damage may be detected with blood work and, fortunately, values often return to normal when the drug is discontinued.

All "medications"—prescription, over the counter, and herbs—have the **potential** to interact with other medications **and even foods.** To avoid possible life-threatening interactions, it is critical that your veterinarian know **all** medications your rabbit is taking, including herbs and supplements. Depending on the substances being combined, interactions can lead to new side effects, increase the **intensity** of common side-effects, magnify the effect of a medication, or decrease the effectiveness of a medication. Some interactions can be avoided simply by staggering the times at which the various medications are given. In other cases, your veterinarian may choose to change one of the medications to avoid any problematic interaction.

Your rabbit's medical history plays an important role in determining the safety of a given treatment **for your rabbit.** How the body processes a particular medication may make a drug that is normally safe a poor choice for your rabbit. For example, drugs that are processed primarily by the kidneys or liver may be a poor choice for a rabbit known to have damage to that organ. It is also important for your veterinarian to be aware of **any** medications your rabbit has reacted poorly to in the past. This information may steer her away from drugs in the same class or drugs that the body processes in a similar manner.

All of the above are reasons that you should **always** consult a qualified rabbit veterinarian and give medications only under her supervision. Carefully follow her instructions about dose, frequency, and combining medications. Be sure to report any unusual symptoms or behavior to your veterinarian as soon as you notice them. Be diligent about scheduling follow-up appointments to check clinical signs, discuss any concerns, and perform any necessary diagnostic tests.

Finally, when giving a new medication to your rabbit, it is a good idea to give the first dose when you will be home for a while to monitor his reaction. For example, give a morning dose when you get up, rather than as you are heading out the door to work. You may also want to give a first dose when your veterinarian will be available—if there is a particular concern about side effects, consider having your veterinarian give the first dose at the clinic and stay until she is comfortable that your rabbit is reacting OK. Extra caution is advised with a new medication if one or more of the following "risk factors" exist:

- The medication frequently causes side effects
- Your rabbit is older (6+years) or in poor health
- Your rabbit is on several medications
- Your rabbit is especially sensitive to medications

Antibiotics/Antifungals

Antibiotics are the most frequently used—and misused—group of drugs for both humans and animals. Overuse and misuse of antibiotics, in humans and animals, can lead to drug-resistant strains of bacteria. It is important for everyone to be aware of the following facts about antibiotics:

1. **Antibiotics are only effective against infections caused by bacteria.** They are ineffective against viral infections (which rabbits rarely get) and can actually exacerbate a yeast infection.

2. **A specific bacteria will not be sensitive to all antibiotics and no single antibiotic is effective against all bacteria.** It is critical to do culture and sensitivity (C&S) tests when a bacterial infection is suspected. The culture portion of a C&S identifies the type of bacteria while the sensitivity portion identifies the drugs that are effective (and equally important, ineffective) against the bacteria.

3. **It is critical to give your rabbit the entire course of antibiotic therapy prescribed.** Do not stop giving the medication—no matter how much your rabbit hates taking it—just because symptoms have gone away. Failure to complete the full course of antibiotics is one of the main causes of drug-resistant strains of bacteria. If your veterinarian advises discontinuing a particular antibiotic because of side-effects, she will probably prescribe another drug. If not, ask if antibiotic therapy should be continued. For severe or persistent infections, antibiotics may be

continued for several weeks after all symptoms have disappeared. Be sure you understand and follow your veterinarian's instructions!

4. **Antibiotics pose a special threat to rabbits who have a very sensitive GI system with a very delicate balance of "gut flora" that can easily be disrupted by antibiotic therapy.** Any changes in your rabbit's appetite or fecals/cecals while on antibiotics should be discussed immediately with your veterinarian. Depending on the severity of the reaction and the other drugs to which the infection is sensitive, she may choose to switch to a different antibiotic or she may prescribe equine Probios® or Bene-bac® supplement (given a couple of hours before or after the antibiotic) to help restore the balance of flora in the GI system. **Note:** Some veterinarians may tell you to give yogurt; however, yogurt may cause additional problems in some rabbits (since a rabbit's GI system is not used to digesting dairy products).

5. **Your veterinarian may want to do a follow-up cytology or culture a week or two after discontinuing antibiotic therapy.** This is an excellent way to ensure that the infection is completely cleared up. It is not unusual for an opportunistic bacteria such as *Pseudomonas aeruginosa* to occur as a secondary infection, requiring a new course of therapy with a different antibiotic. *Pseudomonas aeruginosa* can also mutate and become resistant to the antibiotic being used, so a repeat culture and sensitivity may be necessary.

Veterinarians often prescribe a broad-spectrum antibiotic in cases where bacterial infection is suspected but cannot be confirmed (e.g., presence of a fever with absence of anything that can be cultured) or while awaiting the results of C&S. For severe or persistent infections, she may prescribe two systemic antibiotics (usually from two different classes) that are known to have a synergistic effect when given together. It may also be necessary to prescribe two antibiotics if the culture/sensitivity identifies two bacteria that are sensitive to completely different groups of drugs or if the only antibiotic effective against both bacteria is one that is not safe for rabbits.

Systemic Antibiotics

Systemic antibiotics are given either orally or by injection. This section describes the following classes of antibiotics, discusses their relative safety in rabbits, and lists specific drugs (generic and brand names) that have been used successfully in rabbits:

- Quinolones
- Sulfonamides
- Chloramphenicol
- Aminoglycosides
- Tetracyclines
- Penicillin
- Cephalasporins
- Macrolides

Note that drugs within a class cannot be used interchangeably. A particular bacteria may be sensitive to one drug in a class and resistant to all others. Also note that new antibiotics—including new classes of drugs—are being developed on an ongoing basis. Because a rabbit's GI system is so easily upset by antibiotics, new classes of drugs and new drugs within a class—even one that is generally well tolerated—should be approached with caution.

Quinolones

Antibiotics in this class are generally tolerated well by adult rabbits and are considered relatively safe for long-term use. These drugs do not cross the blood/brain barrier well, so are generally ineffective against infections in the brain. A small number of rabbits have developed neurological symptoms after long-term (a year or more) use of these drugs or when receiving high doses of the drug. If your rabbit experiences neurological symptoms, consult your veterinarian immediately.

The most common side-effects reported from short-term (less than three months) use of quinolones are mild diarrhea and slightly decreased appetite. Report any side effects to your veterinarian promptly. Appetite changes should be monitored closely and significant decreases may require lowering the antibiotic dose or changing to a different drug. Decreased appetite may worsen with longer-term use.

The effect of quinolones on young rabbits is not known. However, since some quinolones have caused joint problems in growing dogs, many veterinarians prefer to use sulfa drugs on rabbits under six months old.

The most frequently used quinolones are:

- Baytril® (Enrofloxacin)
- Dicural® (Difloxacin hydrochloride)
- Cipro® (Ciprofloxacin)
- Maxaquin® (Lomefloxacin hydrochloride)
- Orbax® (Orbafloxacin)

Baytril is available in tablet and injectable forms and the injectable form can also be given orally. Oral Baytril now comes in both the original, unflavored tablets and in a new liver-flavored tablet for dogs and cats. If your rabbit is given Baytril tablets, make sure they are **unflavored.**

Some caretakers actually find it less stressful (to both human and rabbit) to give Baytril by injection instead of orally. The disadvantage of injections is that repeated injections of Baytril may be painful and injections given **into** the skin (instead of through the skin) can cause sterile abscesses at the injection site.

Sulfonamides

The combination drug trimethoprim and sulfamethoxazole (marketed as TMZ-SMZ®, Bactrim® or Septra®) is generally as well tolerated as the quinolones and crosses the blood/brain barrier more readily. These are often the drug of choice for bacterial infections in young rabbits (< six months). Side-effects—diarrhea and slight decrease in appetite—are similar in frequency and intensity to the quinolones.

Chloramphenicol

Chloramphenicol is an excellent antibiotic for rabbits. It has minimal side-effects (GI problems, similar to the quinolones), crosses the blood/brain barrier, and is effective against many organisms that are resistant to the quinolones. Chloramphenicol may be difficult for your veterinarian to locate because it has caused aplastic anemia in a very small number of humans, simply from contact with the drug. Caretakers who give chloramphenicol should use disposable gloves when preparing and administering this drug.

Aminoglycosides

Until recently, the aminoglycosides Amikacin and Gentocin® (Gentamicin) were normally prescribed only for very short-term use (three to five days) because of potential kidney damage and were often given with a longer course of another antibiotic such as Baytril®. My Smokey was a real exception when, in 1996, he received Amikacin injections twice a week for more than two months.

Since the first printing of <u>Rabbit Health 101</u> in July 2000, a number of vets across the country have safely used Amikacin on rabbits for several months at a time. Years ago my Murray began fighting recurring ear infections that consistently cultured pseudomonas sensitive **only** to Amikacin. He has received daily injections for two to three months at a time—several times now—with no signs of kidney damage. When Murray is on Amikacin I give him daily fluids and I inject the Amikacin into the fluid pocket which reduces the discomfort of the injection itself. We also closely monitor BUN and Creatinine levels, checking them at least monthly while he is on Amikacin.

Since aminoglycosides can cause kidney damage they should **not** be used in rabbits known to have kidney disease. It is now felt that once daily dosing provides therapeutic drug levels with less potential for kidney damage.

Tetracyclines

Tetracyclines such as doxycycline (brand name Vibramycin®) and oxytetracycline are generally safe for rabbits. However, over the years, many breeders have added tetracyclines to their rabbits' water as a prophylaxis. As a result, many bacteria found in rabbits are resistant to tetracyclines.

Penicillin

All forms of **oral** penicillins, especially the semisynthetic penicillin derivatives such as Amoxicillin and Ampicillin, can be deadly to your rabbit. Oral penicillins destroy the good gut flora and can kill your rabbit shortly after administration of the drug, or up to three weeks after the drug has been taken. **Never accept a prescription for oral penicillin for your rabbit.**

Injectable forms of Penicillin G (Pen-G), a **natural** penicillin, are relatively safe for rabbits and can be an excellent treatment for abscesses and other infections **caused by bacteria that are sensitive to Pen-G.** The most common Pen-G prescribed for rabbits is the combination of Pen-G Benzathine and Pen-G Procaine, two long-acting forms of the drug. The procaine Pen-G releases the penicillin more rapidly and reaches higher concentrations in the blood; the benzathine releases the penicillin more slowly and has a more prolonged effect but does not reach as high a concentration. Some conditions respond better to Pen-G procaine alone than to the combination product. The potassium and sodium salts of Pen-G are released even more rapidly for immediate, high concentrations of penicillin. Only your veterinarian can determine whether injectible penicillin is an appropriate treatment for your rabbit and, if so, the appropriate form, dose, frequency, and duration of treatment. Factors that will influence her decision include your rabbit's disease, medical history, general health, and other medications.

Bicillin® is the **human** brand name for the procaine/benazathine combination of Pen-G. There are many veterinary brands of this combination which is often referred to generically as "bicillin" (lowercase b) by rabbit owners, many of whom believe it is a "miracle drug" for treating abscesses. If your rabbit has an abscess that has cultured sensitive to penicillin or one that cannot safely be removed surgically or cultured, your veterinarian may want to consider treatment with bicillin. The treatment protocol is available online at http://moorelab.sbs.umass.edu/~mrosenfield/bicillin/

Like humans, a small number of rabbits experience severe allergic reactions (anaphylactic shock) to penicillin. Your veterinarian should show you how to give the injections and should monitor your rabbit after the first dose for signs of anaphylactic shock. Make sure you know how to recognize and respond appropriately to a severe allergic reaction, just in case your rabbit reacts to a later dose.

Cephalosporins

First-generation cephalosporins (e.g., Cephalexin®) have been used safely in rabbits, though they are not usually a veterinarian's first choice. The injectable form of Naxcel® (ceftiofur sodium), developed for treating Pasteurella in cattle, has been used successfully used in some stubborn cases of head-tilt. Naxcel beads have also been used successfully as packing for abscesses after surgery. Rabbits on oral cephalosporins should be monitored for changes in appetite and fecals/cecals. Treatment with equine Probios® or Bene-bac® a couple of hours before or after dosing will help reduce the GI effects.

Note: Second- and third-generation cephalosporins should **not** be given **orally** to rabbits.

Macrolides

Most macrolides (e.g. erythromycin) are toxic and should not be prescribed for rabbits. However, **injectible** Tylan® (tylosin) has been used safely in rabbits. Some veterinarians have also recently reported success treating rabbits with Zithromax® (azithromycin), a derivative of erythromycin. If your veterinarian feels Tylan® or Zithromax® is the right antibiotic for your rabbit's condition, it is important to monitor him closely for GI side-effects such as diarrhea. **Because Propulsid® can be deadly when given with erythromycin, rabbits taking Tylan or Zithromax should not be given Propulsid.**

Systemic Antifungals

Nizoral® (Ketoconazole) tablets have been safely and effectively used to treat yeast infections in rabbits. Medication is given orally, once a day, for a period of 21–24 days. Nizoral is often combined with topical treatments (discussed below) to treat severe yeast infections in the ears.

Over time, Nizoral can cause liver damage and should not be used in rabbits known to have liver disease. It can sometimes cause a decrease in appetite—consult your veterinarian if you notice any change in your rabbit's appetite while on this medication. According to <u>The Physician's Desk Reference</u>, **Nizoral and Propulsid® should not be given at the same time.**

Topical Antibiotics and Antifungals

Topical treatments are frequently prescribed alone when there is only a slight discharge from the eyes or ears or for treatment of surface wounds. They may also be prescribed in conjunction with systemic antibiotics for more serious infections. Some eye and ear preparations contain Dexamethasone, a steroid that helps reduce inflammation. Steroids should be used only when your veterinarian feels it necessary.

Topical antibiotics and antifungals generally fall into one of three categories:

- Ophthalmic (eye) preparations
- Otic (ear) preparations
- General wound care

Eye **drops** are sometimes prescribed for use in the ears. **Eye ointments should never be used in the ears and ear drops should never be used in the eyes.**

Ophthalmic (eye) preparations

Ophthalmic preparations come in both drop and ointment form. Some veterinarians prefer ointments, feeling they stay in the eye better. Others prefer drops because ointments cause the fur around the eyes to become matted, making it more difficult to tell if the discharge has stopped.

Eye drops that have been safe and effective for rabbits include:

*   Gentocin®
*   Gentocin Durafilm (Gentamicin Sulfate—includes a steroid)
*   Ciloxan® Ophthalmic Solution (Ciprofloxacin HCl)
*   Neomycin and Polymyxin B Sulfates and Dexamethasone Ophthalmic Solution
*   Neomycin and Polymyxin B Sulfates and Gramicidin Ophthalmic Solution

Eye ointments include:

*   Neobacimyx® Ophthalmic Ointment (Bacitracin-Neomycin-Polymyxin)
*   Chloramphenicol Ophthalmic Ointment
*   Gentocin®

Otic (ear) Preparations

Ear drops may be antibiotic, antifungal, or both. Antibiotic drops that have been used successfully in rabbits include:

*   Gentocin Otic Solution (Gentamicin Sulfate with Betamethasone Valerate)
*   Neomycin and Polymyxin B Sulfates and Hydrocortisone Otic Solution
*   Conofite®
*   Coly-mycin
*   Tresaderm® (thiabendazole, dexamethasone, neomycin sulfate solution)
*   Baytril® Otic (enrofloxacin/silver sulfadiazine)

Silvadene (Silver Sulfadiazine or SSD for short) is also effective against both yeast and many types of bacteria. Veterinarians who are comfortable compounding may mix the antibiotic they are using to systemically treat an ear infection (e.g. Amikacin) with SSD for use in the ears. Dexamethasone may also be added to SSD, either alone or with an antibiotic, to treat inflammation. (**Note:** Veterinarians are not allowed to compound for "bulk resale" but may legally compound for an individual patient.)

TrizEDTA® is an ear-cleaning solution that appears to inhibit the growth of some bacteria including pseudomonas. Zymox® is an enzymatic ear-cleaning solution that also seems to inhibit the growth of both bacteria and yeast. Zymox is available with or without hydrocortisone. Both products have been used in rabbits with recurring ear infections and seem to increase the time between flare-ups.

General Wound Care

Neosporin® (Polymyxin B sulfate, Bacitracin Zinc, and Neomycin) ointment can be safely used to treat minor wounds in rabbits. Neosporin Plus®, which contains Lidocaine, should **not** be used. Although Neosporin is available over-the-counter, you should consult a veterinarian when using this product. Bactoderm® is a good veterinary antibacterial ointment which your veterinarian may prefer to Neosporin. She may also prescribe Panalog, which contains a steroid, or Pyoben Gel for general wound care. Balmax, A+D, and Desitin Ointment (available in the baby section of your drug or grocery store) may be used for treating skin irritation caused by urine scald. These products protect the skin from wetness and helps it heal.

Analgesics

Appropriate use of analgesics (pain medicines) can help speed up a rabbit's recovery from many medical conditions, including surgery, GI stasis, and dental problems. Effective pain management will usually cause a rabbit to regain his appetite sooner, thus keeping the GI moving. Long-term use of pain medications may be appropriate for rabbits suffering from chronic problems such as arthritis, cancer, kidney and liver disease.

The first step in pain management for your rabbit is to recognize that he is in pain. Signs of pain include:

- Sitting in a hunched position
- Lack of movement, slow or awkward movement, or limping
- Loss of appetite
- Loud tooth grinding (as opposed to tooth purring)
- Unusual aggression or irritability
- Hiding, especially facing a corner

If you think your rabbit is in pain, discuss the problem with your veterinarian as soon as possible. If a problem occurs in the middle of the night or on a Sunday, as it often does, and you have given pain medication before, it may be appropriate to give a dose or two until your regular veterinarian is available for consultation. Remember that pain is almost always a **symptom** of an underlying medical problem. Appropriate pain medications and treatment plans vary greatly depending on the underlying cause of the pain, its expected duration (is this an acute or chronic condition?), and other medications your rabbit is on. The most commonly prescribed analgesics fall into one of two categories:

- Narcotics
- Non-steroidal anti-inflammatory drugs (NSAIDS)

Narcotics

Narcotics are extremely effective analgesics which also produce a sedative effect. Those most commonly used in rabbits are Buprenex® (buprenorphine) and Torbugesic® (butorphanol). Veterinarians often use these drugs for rabbits just before, during, and/or immediately after surgery. Narcotics are generally given by injection and are controlled substances. Some veterinarians limit the use of narcotics to the hospital, while others may prescribe them for short-term use at home.

NSAIDS

Non-steroidal anti-inflammatory drugs (NSAIDS) decrease swelling and inflammation in addition to reducing pain. NSAIDS include both over-the-counter and prescription medications in a wide variety of strengths. Over-the-counter NSAIDS that have been safely used in rabbits include aspirin and ibuprofen. Acetaminophen (the active ingredient in Tylenol®) is not recommended for rabbits.

Prescription NSAIDS that have been safely used in rabbits include Banamine® (flunixin meglumine), Rimadyl® (carprofen), and Metacam® (meloxicam).

Banamine is an injectable NSAID for horses—a species with a GI system similar to a rabbit's. Veterinarians who see primarily dogs and cats often hesitate to prescribe Banamine because of its side-effects in these species. However, top rabbit specialists consider it to be particularly effective against soft-tissue pain, including intestinal pain. It may also help prevent toxins from forming in the intestines. **Note:** Banamine can be combined with Torbugesic® for rabbits in severe pain.

Rimadyl is an oral NSAID that has been used long-term (several months) on rabbits with a variety of chronic illnesses including cancer, arthritis, and kidney failure. It is less effective than Banamine or Torbugesic against soft-tissue pain, but is effective against joint and bone pain.

Metacam (meloxicam) is a newer NSAID. The human version, Mobic®, was approved in April 2000 for the treatment of arthritis pain and inflammation. Veterinarians are beginning to use it in rabbits to treat both chronic pain such as arthritis and post-surgical pain.

If NSAIDS are used long-term, they should be given at the lower end of the dosage range and the rabbit should be watched for signs of gastric ulcers. Although this has not been a common problem in rabbits, as it has been in other species, fewer rabbits have received long-term treatment with NSAIDS. Except in rare cases, NSAIDS should **not** be given **with** corticosteriods because this combination increases the potential for ulcers and other GI problems.

As with humans, the analgesic that works wonders for one rabbit may do nothing for another. Effective pain management may require trying different drugs and adjusting dosages to meet the needs of the individual rabbit and medical condition being treated. This requires teamwork between a skilled veterinarian and a perceptive caretaker. Meanwhile, caregivers can minimize their rabbit's discomfort with careful handling and lots of extra TLC.

Steroids

Steroids usually are prescribed only for short-term use. The following steroids have been used in treating a variety of rabbit ailments:

Dexamethasone is an adrenocortical steroid used to reduce inflammation and/or pain from a variety of conditions including severe ear infections, arthritis, and allergic reactions. Dexamethasone may be used as a component in eye or ear drops or it may be given as a one-dose injection.

Prednisone is a glucocorticoid (a type of adrenocortical steroid) used to reduce inflammation and/or pain from a variety of conditions, including severe ear infections, arthritis, and allergic reactions. It is also used as a basic form of chemotherapy in cases of cancer in rabbits. It generally makes the patient more comfortable, thus improving the appetite. Prednisone is known to have immunosuppressive effects; therefore, your veterinarian should exercise caution when prescribing prednisone for long-term use or for rabbits with compromised immune systems. It is sometimes used in conjunction with antibiotic therapy for rabbits battling severe infections. When discontinuing treatment with prednisone, the dose should always be tapered down gradually.

Winstrol is an anabolic steroid used to stimulate appetite in ailing or elderly rabbits who are losing weight. It should not be used in conjunction with other steroids.

Note: Except in rare cases steroids should not be used in conjunction with NSAIDS.

GI Medications

Phazyme® or any pediatric suspension of simethicone drops acts mechanically to break up gas bubbles and pass them through the GI tract. Simethicone is not absorbed by the intestine and is safe to give if you even **suspect** your rabbit is suffering from gas. However, it should not be used every day for more than a week or two.

Questran® (Cholestyramine) may be prescribed if overgrowth of clostridia is confirmed or even suspected. Questran binds to the toxins produced by clostridia, allowing them to be eliminated in the feces. Your dosing instructions for Questran should include mixing it with a **generous** amount of water. **Be sure to follow these instructions** since Questran can dehydrate the intestines if given with too little water. Questran is not absorbed by the body and is very safe if used as directed.

Lactated Ringer's Solution (subcutaneous) will often make a bunny feel better even if he is not obviously dehydrated. LRS also helps maintain electrolyte balance, which is vital for proper muscle function, including GI muscles!

Reglan® (metaclopramide) is an intestinal motility drug that stimulates contractions in the upper GI and has anti-nausea properties. **Propulsid®** (cisapride) is a gastrointestinal motility drug that accelerates stomach emptying while stimulating contractions in the lower esophagus and intestines. Because Reglan and Propulsid affect different portions of the intestinal tract, they seem to have a synergistic effect when used together. The effect of these drugs on cecum motility is not known.

Caution: Propulsid was removed from general availability for humans because of potentially serious heart-related side-effects. While there is no direct evidence that these problems apply to rabbits, my Murray **did** develop heart problems after being on Propulsid for three years. However, he very likely would not have survived those three years without motility drugs, and Propulsid has fewer known central nervous system side-effects than Reglan. If your rabbit requires long-term use of a motility drug, discuss the risks and benefits of the two drugs with your veterinarian. **Note:** According to The Physician's Desk Reference, **Propulsid should not be given with some antifungal drugs including Nizoral® (Ketoconazole), with some antibiotics (Zithromax® and Tylan®), or with the herb Hawthorn (see the section on herbs for more detail).**

Sulfasalazine is a combination analgesic and antibiotic often used to treat colic in horses. It soothes the inflamed intestinal lining and kills harmful bacteria.

Sucralfate is a human ulcer treatment that binds to the ulcerated sites to form a protective barrier along the stomach/intestinal lining. It has safely been given to treat ulcers diagnosed during GI surgery and has been used as a prophylactic in rabbits requiring long-term use of NSAIDS. It should be given twice a day for at least three to four weeks, and it is **extremely** important not to miss a dose, since Sucralfate works cumulatively. Sucralfate works best on an empty stomach and interacts with some antibiotics, specifically quinolones, so it is **especially** important to carefully follow your veterinarian's instructions for giving this medication. **Prilosec®** (omeprazole) is another ulcer drug that has been used safely to treat suspected ulcers in rabbits. Simethecone should not be given with Sucralfate or Prilosec.

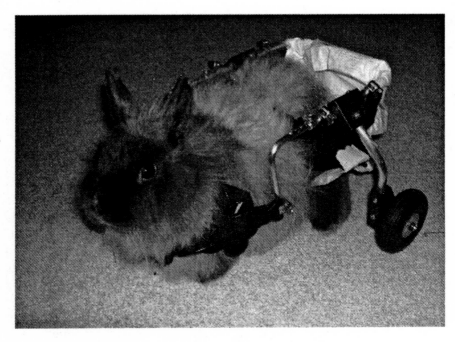

JB was found as a stray on a Texas university campus with a broken back. She had puncture wounds around the area of the break from a predator and was full of maggots when she arrived at the shelter. A volunteer saw that she had a will to live, rescued her from being euthanized, and took her to a rescuer in the Dallas area. After 3-4 weeks of medications and twice daily hydrotherapy, her wounds healed. She is now a happy, independent rabbit thanks to her cart from Doggon Wheels. (Photo by Lisa Hafer)

ALTERNATIVE MEDICINE

WARNING: The topics discussed in this chapter should not be interpreted as "home remedies," should never substitute for a visit to your veterinarian, and should not be used without first consulting your rabbit's primary veterinarian.

This chapter discusses alternative medicine techniques that have been successfully used either in conjunction with traditional medicine or, on occasion, alone. These treatments are often described as holistic because both examination and treatment focus on the patient as a whole rather than being narrowly focused on treatment of a specific symptom. This holistic approach reduces the probability that treatment of one symptom or disease will create a problem in a different part of the body. Because holistic medicine is aimed at restoring a **balance** within the body and stimulating the body to heal itself, it can sometimes succeed when traditional medicine fails. This is particularly true of problems for which the "root cause" cannot be determined. More information on alternative veterinary medicine, including a list of holistic veterinarians by state, is available at http://www.altvetmed.com.

The most widely practiced holistic techniques are acupuncture/acupressure, chiropractic, and herbs—all of which have been used on my own rabbits. The last section of this chapter briefly describes other alternative therapies including Homeopathy, Flower Essences, Reiki, TTouch, and massage. I have also included the topic of Animal Communicators in this section, because I have found Murray's communicator to be an especially valuable "alternative" resource in identifying and treating his medical problems.

If you feel your rabbit may benefit from the holistic treatments described here, discuss the possibility with your primary veterinarian **before** trying them. Doctors (both human and animal) vary in their acceptance of alternative medicine. Even if your veterinarian does not think there is any chance the technique will help, ask if she has any reason to think it will **harm** your bunny or interfere with other treatments. This is especially important with herbs. Remember, just because herbal remedies are "natural", this is no guarantee that they are totally safe. Also, as herbs are being used more widely, more interactions between herbs and traditional medications are being discovered.

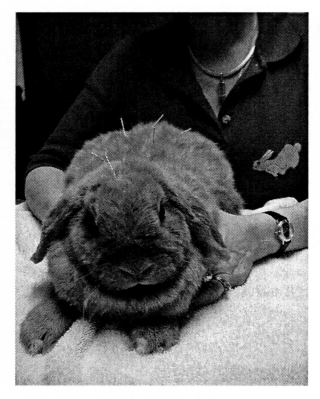

Murray's health problems have been helped by a combination of alternative med-icine and traditional western medicine. The first time he tooth-purred for me was during an acupuncture treatment. (Photo by Randy Kidd, DVM)

Herbal Treatments

Unlike prescription and over-the-counter drugs, herbal products are not regulated by the FDA or any other government agency. This makes it difficult to compare prices across brands or even determine the amount of "active ingredient" in a product. Although some holistic vets use Chinese herbs, my holistic vet prefers "western" herbs to avoid another level of variability (foreign sources) and because imported herbs must be treated for insects. He recommends buying herbs in their most "natural" form and, whenever possible, letting his patients consume what they need. Note: If you use fresh herbs from your yard, be certain that they have **not** been sprayed with harmful chemicals and that they are not near the road where exhaust particulates can collect on them. Always wash fresh herbs thoroughly. Although herbs are "natural," they can still interact with other drugs. If your rabbit has health problems or is on **any** medication, discuss herbs with your vet **before** giving them to your rabbit.

For rabbits, herbal treatments can be separated into two categories:

- Herbs that many rabbits eat willingly and which **may** have beneficial medicinal properties. These may already be a part of your rabbit's diet or can easily be included as part of salads, offered as treats, or made available for chewing.

- Herbs with known medicinal properties which are usually administered as medicine.

Herbs As Part of the Diet and Toy Box

The herbs in this section may be offered to rabbits either as part of their regular diet, as special treats, or as something to play with or chew on. Note that not all rabbits will like all the herbs listed below. If your holistic veterinarian feels your rabbit needs one of the herbs listed in this section and your rabbit refuses to touch it, you can always purchase a capsule or non-alcoholic tincture or extract and administer as a medicine.

Birch is said to act as a diuretic, to lessen inflammation, and to relieve pain. Offer your rabbit birch twigs to chew on. **Parts used:** fresh stems.

Borage leaves are useful for gently strengthening adrenal function, which is particularly important in pets that have undergone steroid therapy; so offer some fresh leaves to your rabbit to nibble on. Topically, the leaves can be applied as a compress for minor skin irritations. **Note:** Dried leaves lose their medicinal qualities rather quickly, so freshness is important. **Parts used:** leaves and seed oil (capsules).

Chamomile is a non-toxic de-wormer. While it does not work as fast as other herbal de-wormers, it offers anti-inflammatory activity that helps counteract the effect parasites often have on intestinal mucosa. It has constricting and strengthening effects on smooth muscles throughout the body, including heart, bladder, and especially the uterus. It also has properties as an appetite stimulant, antispasmodic, digestive aid, gas reliever, diuretic, sedative, nerve tonic, and sleep aid. It is used as a remedy for a variety of GI upsets, fever, aches and pains, anxiety, and insomnia. Topically, it can be used to treat skin irritations from insect bites, allergies and fungal infections and to clean the eyes (make an infusion). **Note:** Some animals are allergic so check first by applying a small amount to the skin before feeding it to your bunny. **Do not use during pregnancy. Parts used:** flowers. **Preparations:** fresh herb, infusion, tincture or salve.

Cranberry is a good source of vitamin C and is helpful for treating urinary tract infections. Although fresh cranberry is considered bitter by humans, some rabbits will eat it willingly—try cutting them in half to reduce the frustration associated with trying to eat a round food that tries to run away! **Parts used:** fruit.

Dandelion contains vitamins A, C, K, D, and B-complex, trace minerals, and protein. The root is useful as a liver tonic, which cleanses the bloodstream and gently increases the production of bile so as not to irritate an inflamed condition. The leaves have a diuretic effect which is useful in treatment of congestive heart failure, pulmonary edema, arthritis, kidney stones and gall bladder disease; but unlike diuretic medicines, it supplies the body with much needed potassium. Flowers have weak analgesic qualities. The Vitamin K may be useful in treating blood disorders where clotting factors are involved. **Parts used:** all parts of the plant are medicinal. **Preparations:** infusion, tincture or fresh herb.

Dill has weak antibacterial properties. It is good for gingivitis, relieves flatulence, and possesses volatile oils that increase the production of cancer-fighting enzymes. **Parts used:** leaves, flowers and seeds. **Preparations:** fresh herb, infusion or tincture.

Fennel promotes the function of the kidneys and liver. It has gentle anti-gas and antispasmodic properties and may increase appetite. An infusion made from the leaves makes an effective rinse for fleas. **Caution:** fennel may cause a photosensitive reaction in some animals. **Parts used:** seeds, leaves and roots. **Preparations:** fresh or dried leaves, seeds or roots; tincture or infusion.

Ginger improves digestion and circulation and has an anti-inflammatory action. It is useful in treating arthritis and makes other herbs more easily assimilated. **Parts used:** root. **Preparations:** decoction.

Grapefruit seed extract is antimicrobial and is used with Echinacea and Goldenseal to treat respiratory illnesses and viral infections. It also augments the healing ability of other herbs. **Parts used:** seeds. **Preparations:** standardized extract.

Hawthorn is an herb that is often described as a "tonic for the heart." It has been effective in the treatment of chest pain, congestive heart failure (CHF), arrhythmia, and blood pressure (whether high or low). It increases coronary and myocardial blood flow by dilating and relaxing coronary blood vessels, thus increasing blood flow without increasing pressure. In addition, it has a mild diuretic effect. Its mechanism of action is believed to be similar to that of Class III Anti-arrhythmics, which slow electrical impulses in the heart by blocking the heart's potassium channels. **Warning:** According **to the** <u>PDR for Herbal Medicines</u>**, Hawthorn should not be given with Propulsid®** (cisapride) because both medications inhibit the inward flow of potassium channels. It should also be given **cautiously** with prescription heart medications. **Lower** doses of ACE inhibitors may be appropriate with hawthorn since hawthorn has similar effects. **Hypertension** has been reported when hawthorn has been used with some beta-blockers. **Parts used:** berries and buds. **Preparations:** decoction, fresh/dried berries.

Kava kava induces physical and mental relaxation without causing sedation. It can help prolong the benefits of chiropractic adjustments and has been beneficial to rabbits suffering from head tilt. If the actual root is available at your health food store, it can be mixed in with pellets and many rabbits will eat it willingly. **Warning: May be damaging to the liver if used in excess.** Parts used: root.

Papaya stimulates the appetite and aids digestion. **Parts used:** fresh or dried fruit (unsweetened).

Parsley relieves gas and stimulates normal GI activity. It is useful as a diuretic, especially in rheumatoid conditions. It helps bladder, kidney, liver, and lung functions and is said to contain a substance that inhibits multiplication of tumor cells. It may help boost kidney function in early-onset renal failure. **Parts used:** leaves, seeds and roots. **Preparations:** fresh herb or infusion.

Peppermint can be used for gas, diarrhea and as a digestive aid. It encourages bile production and improves liver and gallbladder function. It is a great stimulant and antispasmodic and also soothes the nervous system. **Caution:** Peppermint should not be used with homeopathic remedies as it may counteract their effects. **Parts used:** leaves, stems. **Preparations:** fresh herb or infusion.

Plantain lubricates and soothes internal mucous membranes and is an anti-inflammatory, making it especially good for bladder and gastrointestinal inflammation. It slows or stops bleeding/hemorrhaging and when used as a poultice, will help clean the blood after poisonous bites or stings. **Parts used:** the whole plant. **Preparations:** tincture, infusion or applied externally as a poultice.

Raspberry is a mild sedative, diuretic and an excellent source of Vitamin C. An infusion of the leaves can be used to treat mild cases of diarrhea. **Parts used:** leaves. **Preparations:** fresh herb, infusion.

Red clover acts as a blood purifier and relaxant. It may be useful in treating bacterial infections, skin conditions, kidney and liver disease. It can help boost a weakened immune system and may have anti-tumor properties. **Note:** Red clover also acts as an appetite suppressant, so it should be fed with caution to rabbits prone to GI stasis. **Warning:** Red Clover has blood-thinning properties. **Do not use in animals with clotting disorders or bleeding** (either internal or external). Do not use during pregnancy or while nursing. **Parts used:** flowering tops. **Preparations:** fresh herbs, infusion or tincture.

Rosemary fights bacteria, is helpful in treating nasal allergies, relaxes the stomach, and stimulates circulation and digestion. It also helps prevent liver toxicity and may have anticancer and anti-tumor properties. **Parts used:** leaves, stems and flowers. **Preparations:** fresh herbs, infusion or tincture.

Sage stimulates the central nervous system and digestive system. It has antimicrobial properties and is good for treating fungal and bacterial infections of the mouth and digestive tract. **Parts used:** leaves, stems and flowers. **Preparations:** fresh herbs, infusion or tincture. Tea can be added to drinking water.

Spearmint is similar to peppermint but milder in action. It is soothing to the nerves, relieves gas and colic, is a mild diuretic and reduces fluid retention. **Parts used:** leaves, stems. **Preparations:** fresh herb or infusion.

Thyme eliminates gas, helps expel intestinal parasites, and reduces fever, headache, and mucous. It may help with liver disease and respiratory problems including bronchial spasms due to asthma. It can also be used as an antiseptic for the mouth and throat. **Parts used:** leaves, stems and flowers. **Preparations:** fresh herbs, infusion or tincture.

Valerian improves circulation, may be helpful in treating seizures, and acts as a sedative (most effective when given in small doses several times a day for several days). Like kava kava, the root may be available at health food stores. Valerian has an odor that is unpleasant to humans—your rabbit may or may not eat it willingly. **Parts used:** the fall root. **Preparations:** fresh/dried herbs, decoction or tincture.

Willow is an excellent natural pain reliever and fever reducer. Willow baskets, chew rings, and tunnels are available from many bunny-friendly suppliers and make excellent toys for your rabbit. **Parts used:** stems.

Wintergreen relieves pain and inflammation and is an effective remedy for arthritic conditions. The methyl salicylate in the leaves is closely related to salicylic acid (aspirin). **Parts used:** leaves, essential oil. **Preparations:** infusion, ointment.

Medicinal Herbs

The herbs in this section have been used successfully in rabbits for the conditions discussed. They are not **as** readily available in a form that a rabbit will eat willingly as those discussed in the previous section. However, unprocessed versions of these herbs are available at some health food stores (e.g. Wild Oats Community Markets). If you can find this form (usually a root, dried leaf, or seeds), many rabbits will willingly eat these herbs as well, especially if their body needs the herb's healing properties. As with the herbs listed in the previous section, if you cannot find a form your rabbit will willingly eat, you can purchase a capsule or non-alcoholic tincture or extract and administer as a medicine.

Note: Echinacea and Goldenseal (or Oregon Grape root), discussed below, may be used separately or together (under your veterinarian's supervision) in conjunction with antibiotic therapy to treat resistant or recurring infections.

Astragalus stimulates T-cell activity and interferon production, and raises white blood cell counts. It is antibacterial, anti-inflammatory, strengthens the body against viral infections and increases stamina. It also strengthens kidney circulation, making it useful in early stages of kidney infection or renal failure. It can be used to boost energy levels in debilitated rabbits and is important in maintaining immune system balance when undergoing chemotherapy or radiation treatment. **Parts used:** Mature roots (at least three years old). **Preparations:** decoction, tincture.

Bugleweed slows the release of the thyroid hormone thyroxin, which makes it useful in treating **mild** cases of hyperthyroidism—however, **it should not be used with thyroid medications.** It is helpful in heart and vascular system disorders, strengthening the heartbeat and slowing a rapid pulse. It is also effective in helping the body rid itself of excess fluid in the lungs and can be used as a cough suppressant. **Warning:** Bugleweed is believed to suppress a cough even if the suppression isn't conducive to healing, i.e., when the body needs to expel excess mucous from the lungs. **Do not use in pregnant or nursing females. Parts used:** leaves, stems and flowers. **Preparations:** alcohol or glycerin tincture.

Burdock Root is a nutritious liver tonic, which also helps to clean and build the blood. A decoction made from the root and applied externally and taken internally is a specific treatment for chronic or acute psoriasis or eczema. Because of its anti-inflammatory qualities, it is helpful in treating arthritis, inflammatory kidney and bladder diseases, and other conditions that are a result of poor waste elimination. It is diuretic and will help remove mutagenic substances such as pesticides and air-borne pollutants from the bloodstream **before** they can harm the body. It is also a free-radical scavenger. It is gentle enough to use with existing liver and kidney disease. **Parts used:** root. **Preparations:** decoction or glycerin tincture.

Catnip is a gentle gas-reliever and antispasmodic and mild sedative. It is good for high-strung rabbits or for stressful events such as trips to the vet. **Warning: Do not** feed your rabbit the seeds. **Do not** feed to pregnant or lactating females. **Parts used:** leaves, stems and flowers before the seeds begin to develop. **Preparations:** fresh/dried herb, infusion or tincture.

Chickweed can be fed as an aid in the removal of hairballs due to its roughage and lubricating abilities. Use chickweed juice, infusion or fresh chickweed herb to soothe an irritated stomach lining. The infusion or mashed fresh herb can be used as a poultice for skin irritations due to dryness. **Caution:** eating a large quantity can have a laxative effect. **Parts used:** fresh leaves, flowers and stems. **Preparations:** feed the fresh plant or its fresh juice, an infusion or use an ointment made from it.

Comfrey is a cell proliferant, stimulating the cells around a wound to reproduce more quickly and seal up the wound, and is a soother and healer. It contains PAs (pyrrolizidine alkaloids), so it is **only recommended for external use.** The allantoin in comfrey can stimulate wound healing quite quickly, so it is **crucial** to be certain that the wound is thoroughly cleaned with an antibacterial agent **before** using comfrey in order to prevent the bacteria from being trapped in the wound. **Parts used:** all aboveground parts. **Preparations:** infusion or poultice.

Corn silk is a diuretic, an anti-inflammatory, a bile stimulant and is a specific treatment for chronic inflammation of any part of the urinary tract. It also soothes internal mucous membranes, making it quite helpful in easing the discomfort of kidney and bladder problems. It is very helpful in the early stages of kidney diseases, reducing pain/inflammation and easing the passing of stones. It can either be fed to the rabbit or an infusion can be made of it. **Caution: Do not** use during pregnancy. **Parts used:** silk. **Preparations:** low-alcohol tincture or infusion.

Echinacea boosts the immune system. It stimulates certain white blood cells and has anti-inflammatory, antibacterial, and antiviral properties. It accelerates phagocytosis, the means by which microphages and other antibodies attack and eliminate bacteria. It also stops the production of the enzyme that makes cells vulnerable to attack by invading microbes and makes the invading microbes more vulnerable to antibodies. It is a good treatment for upper respiratory infections (snuffles). **Caution:** Echinacea may interfere with the cancer chemotherapeutic effect of corticosteroids. **Echinacea should not be given continuously.** Carefully follow your veterinarian's recommended schedule (e.g., five days on and two days off **or** 14 days on and seven days off). **Parts used:** entire plant, especially the root. **Preparations:** fresh herb, tincture or decoction.

Eyebright is anti-catarrhal (rids the body of excess mucous), making it a good treatment for allergic rhinitis or respiratory infections. It is also an effective eyewash. **Note: Do not** use during pregnancy or lactation. **Parts used:** above-ground parts. **Preparations:** infusion.

Garlic has antibacterial, antiviral, antifungal and anticancer properties and stimulates the immune system. If your rabbit can tolerate the odor, give a pinch of garlic powder three or four times weekly to benefit their overall health or it may be given as a tincture. For rabbits who won't touch it, applying it on surfaces that they like to chew (but that you would rather that they not) is an effective deterrent. Test a small amount of juice on an inconspicuous surface first to be certain that you will not damage it. **Warning: Do not use in anemic animals.** May increase the risk of bleeding when combined with NSAIDS.

Ginkgo Biloba has a tonic effect on the brain, nervous and vascular system. Gingko improves circulation to the peripheral arteries and small capillaries, increasing blood flow (and thus flow of oxygen) to the brain and kidneys; helps regulate the tone and elasticity of blood vessels, making them stronger and less susceptible to degenerative disease; and increases energy levels in the brain and stimulates the release of various neurotransmitters, many of which regulate constriction of important smooth-muscle tissues throughout the body-such as those of the heart and bladder. Gingko can be used in the treatment of early-stage renal failure, urinary incontinence, seizures, neuralgia, skin problems, chronic digestive upset, cardiac arrhythmia, and behavioral/mood disorders. It may also reduce the risk of stroke and may be used along with other therapies to treat the neurologic symptoms of *e. cuniculi*. **Caution:** Because it inhibits platelet aggregation, it should not be used with blood-thinning drugs or in animals with blood-clotting disorders. While ginkgo improves the body's ability to heal after surgery, its use should be delayed until all risk of postoperative hemorrhage has passed. **Parts used:** leaves. **Preparations:** fresh herbs, capsules or tincture.

Goldenrod is a diuretic and reduces respiratory inflammation, strengthens kidney function, helps eliminate kidney stones, is antibacterial and antifungal and helps stop bleeding. It boosts renal function quickly so it is very helpful in acute cases of nephritis (especially if urination is difficult or has stopped). **Warning:** Goldenrod is **contraindicated** in cases of advanced chronic kidney disease where stimulation of renal function may cause added stress. **ALWAYS consult your holistic veterinarian before using goldenrod. Parts used:** entire plant. **Preparations:** dried herb, tincture or infusion.

Goldenseal strengthens the immune system. It has anti-inflammatory and antimicrobial (bacteria, fungus, and protozoa) properties and may be helpful in fighting *E. cuniculi* as well as a wide variety of bacteria. Because it is also an astringent, it is mildly helpful in drying up excess nasal mucous. Over harvesting has made it rare and quite expensive. Ask your holistic veterinarian about substituting Oregon Grape Root which is also high in berberine. **Parts used:** mostly the roots, but the leaves also have medicinal properties. **Preparations:** infusion, tincture or poultice.

Gravel Root is a diuretic, anti-inflammatory and anti-lithic, preventing or relieving stones in the urinary tract. It aids in expelling small kidney and bladder stones and reduces the pain and inflammation of cystitis. Its diuretic qualities help the body eliminate excess uric acid, making it useful in treating rheumatism. **Parts used:** roots. **Preparations:** decoction or tincture.

Milk Thistle helps take ammonia from the blood, protects both the liver and the kidneys, stimulates the production of new liver cells and can aid in reversing liver damage. It is also important in the treatment of mushroom poisoning, environmental toxins and drug damage. **Preparations:** standardized powder extract or alcohol tincture (a high concentration of alcohol is needed to remove the active constituents, so be cautious of "low-alcohol" tinctures). **Parts used:** seeds.

Oregon Grape Root has properties similar to goldenseal but is more available (not endangered) and is gentler to the GI tract. It increases appetite, aids digestion and is an excellent blood purifier and liver stimulant. **Parts used:** roots. **Preparations:** decoction, tincture.

Uva Ursi is a diuretic and urinary antiseptic. It is recommended for urinary tract infections and kidney problems. Some herbalists report that it has worked on UTI's that have been resistant to antibiotics. You should always consult a veterinarian and follow her instructions if you suspect your bunny has a UTI or kidney problems. However, you may want to offer Uva Ursi in addition to antibiotics. My bunnies with UTI's have eaten it eagerly! **Caution:** May add to GI upset when used with NSAIDS. **Parts used:** leaves. **Preparations:** dried/fresh leaves or infusion.

Wormwood is an anthelmintic, which expels intestinal parasites/worms. It is also a muscle relaxant that is helpful when added to liniments, rubs and poultices. It eases gas and bloating. **Note:** The essential oil (Absinthe) is both toxic and addictive. **Parts used:** leaves. **Preparations:** infusion, poultice or tincture.

Preparation of Herbal Teas and Dosage Guidelines

Preparations of Herbal Teas: An **infusion** is a tea made from the leaves, flowers and fruits of plants. To make an infusion, pour one cup boiling water over one tablespoon herb and steep for ten minutes. A **decoction** is a tea made from the hard or tough parts of plants, such as roots or stems. To make a decoction, add one tablespoon of dried herb to 8-12 ounces of water and low boil for 10-15 minutes.

Note: Store herbal teas in the refrigerator for no more than four days. Additional quantities may be frozen for later use.

Dosage Guidelines. Most herbal tincture dosages are based on weight, i.e., 60-120 drops per 150 pounds of body weight. That would mean that a five pound rabbit would need no more than 2-4 drops (.005-.01 CC) of a tincture several times daily, which makes the concerns over any alcohol in the tincture very small. **Most** herbal teas can be given at a dose of 0.7–1.5 CC several times daily.

King Murray has been treated with a number of herbs over the years. When he was having recurring urinary tract infections, he would eagerly eat the uva ursi leaves I put out for him. When he was receiving regular chiropractic adjustments, I also fed him kava kava on a regular basis. He is not currently receiving any herbal treatments because of the number of drugs he is on and the possibility of herb-drug interactions. (Photo by Kathy Smith)

Acupuncture and Acupressure

Acupuncture and acupressure treatments have been helpful in treating a number of conditions including:

•   Pain resulting from arthritis, spondylosis, and many other conditions
•   Head-tilt symptoms
•   Chronic GI slowdowns
•   Heart, liver, and kidney failure

As stated in the introduction to this section, I am not suggesting acupuncture or acupressure instead of proven traditional treatments. However, you may wish to use them in conjunction with traditional treatments or in cases where traditional treatment is not adequate.

Acupuncture and acupressure are based on the concept that the body has an orderly arrangement of energy lines, called meridians, running through it. Disease occurs when these energy lines are blocked, weakened, or deficient in some way. Acupuncture points are points along these meridians, each of which is associated with a specific part of the body or organ system. Acupuncture points are arranged symmetrically, with corresponding points on the left and right sides of the body.

In acupuncture therapy, special solid metal needles are inserted in the acupuncture point or points that are associated with the physical problems being treated. Needles are left in place for roughly 15 minutes, during which time they stimulate the flow of energy through these points. Despite the use of needles, acupuncture is relatively painless. Occasionally, a rabbit will object to placement of one or two needles in particular. Certain points seem to stimulate this response in most rabbits while others may actually indicate a point that **needs** stimulation. Sometimes a needle can be inserted in the corresponding point on the opposite side of the body without causing the same reaction.

You **may** notice improvement after only one acupuncture treatment, but often it takes three to eight treatments to fairly determine whether acupuncture is benefiting your rabbit. You should be willing to try a minimum of three to four treatments before giving up on the healing possibilities of acupuncture.

Acupressure is based on the same principles as acupuncture and is often described as acupuncture without needles. In acupressure, stimulation of the same acupuncture points is done using gentle finger pressure. Because it is non-invasive, acupressure is something you can learn to do for your rabbit. Your acupuncturist may show you how to do this between acupuncture treatments—if not, ask if this would be helpful!

Many holistic veterinarians combine acupuncture, acupressure, chiropractic, and herbal treatments to treat a variety of conditions. As with all veterinarians, it is important to make sure that your holistic veterinarian has some familiarity with rabbit anatomy.

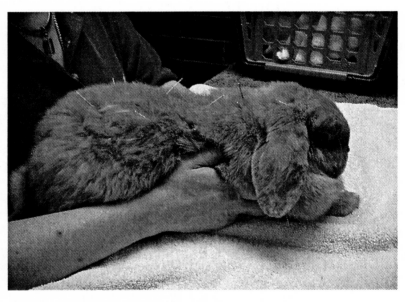

Murray is nearly always relaxed during his acupuncture treatments. In fact, the first time he ever tooth-purred for me was during a treatment. (Photo by Randy Kidd, DVM)

Chiropractic

Chiropractic treatment is based on the concept that pain and many other physical disorders are caused, at least in part, by misalignment of the spine. Chiropractors believe that when spinal vertebrae are properly aligned, impulses from the brain can travel freely through the spinal cord to the body's organ systems, maintaining their healthy function. When there is misalignment, the flow of these impulses is disrupted, leading to pain and other physical ailments. By returning the spine's alignment to its normal state, the nervous system can again function properly and the body can heal itself.

Older bunnies and those requiring frequent handling are likely to benefit from chiropractic treatments. When you look straight at your bunny (not from an angle), carefully observe whether one eye seems higher than the other or one eye seems to bulge more than the other. Both of these are indications that your bunny may benefit from chiropractic treatment.

Because of a rabbit's fragile bone structure, it is especially important that your veterinary chiropractor have experience with rabbits or at least recognize how easily rabbits can be injured by improper handling.

Chiropractic treatment begins with a thorough examination of the rabbit to identify spinal misalignments. Adjustments may include one or more of the following techniques:

- Gentle manipulation to restore proper alignment
- Manipulation of the vertebra with a hand-held, rubber-tipped instrument
- Doctor-assisted stretches
- Gentle massage

Your doctor may show you how to perform the stretches and massages and instruct you to do this at home between treatments. Herbs may also be prescribed to help prolong the effects of the chiropractic adjustments.

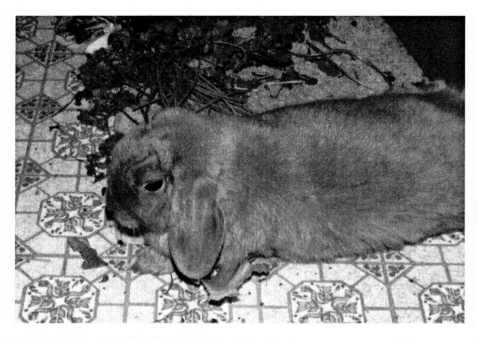

Murray receives regular chiropractic and acupuncture treatments to help manage chronic tooth and GI problems. (Photo by Kathy Smith)

Other Alternative Techniques

Homeopathy

Homeopathy is based on the concept that infinitesimal doses of a substance that would cause a symptom in a healthy patient can be used to treat the same symptom in a sick patient. Homeopathic remedies are believed to stimulate the immune system, encouraging the body to heal itself by strengthening the immune system. Some homeopathic doctors believe that by prescribing treatments that suppress symptoms, traditional medicine has actually helped create chronic ailments by driving the disease deeper into the body's system.

Homeopathic remedies should be used with caution since this type of treatment may cause symptoms to temporarily worsen until the immune system kicks in. For this reason, they are not recommended for life-threatening problems or where a proven, conventional cure is available. However, if you have a trusted holistic veterinarian who understands rabbits, homeopathic remedies may be an option to consider for some ailments, especially if conventional treatment options have been exhausted.

Flower Essences

Flower Essence therapy is based on the principle that many physical conditions and diseases have emotional roots. Rabbits who were rescued from neglectful or abusive situations often have emotional scars. Rabbits are also extremely sensitive to the emotional climate in their current home. If there is stress in your household (as there is in most households today), your rabbit may benefit from flower essence therapy. Flower essences may be given by adding two to four drops to a bowl of water or by placing a drop or two on the top of the rabbit's head.

Rescue Remedy, a combination of five flower essences, is used by many rescuers as an all-purpose treatment for stress. For more specific problems, my holistic vet recommends carefully observing your rabbit's behavior and attitude and matching that to the list of essences and their effects (such a list should be available at stores that sell the flower essences). If you have a close bond with the rabbit being treated, trust your instincts to steer you to the proper flower essence for the condition you are observing.

Reiki

Reiki is an ancient healing technique based on belief in a Universal Life Energy, which is all around us and has healing powers. Reiki practitioners have been attuned by a Reiki Master to be a channel for transferring the life force's healing energy to others. There are different levels of Reiki training. Practitioners with only Level I training must have physical contact with the patient. Level II training allows the practitioner to direct healing energy without physical contact. Level III Reiki Masters can teach and attune others.

The healing energy of Reiki must be directed at something specific (a specific person or animal **and** a specific problem area such as the GI or ears), but it cannot be directed for a specific **outcome**. It treats the entire person or animal, including mind, body, and spirit and has been used for pain management, healing, relaxation and promoting general well-being.

TTouch

Developed by internationally recognized animal expert, Linda Tellington-Jones, TTouch is a process of awakening the cells in the body to increase body awareness and release tension. The approach is fairly basic: using your fingers and hands you apply various circular patterns with different amounts of pressure. You can use it on the entire body with select patterns being used for specific ailments. TTouch is used for both health and behavioral issues. It deepens the bond between human and animal.

Massage

Massage Therapy, which originated thousands of years ago, has long been used for relaxation, pain management, natural healing, increased circulation and/or mobility. Massage is traditionally the manual manipulation of muscles and soft tissues in the body. The most common use of massage in rabbits is to relieve pain from excessive gas. Massage has been also used to assist in realigning the muscles for rabbits suffering from head tilt.

Animal Communication

When you know your rabbit isn't feeling well, how often have you wished he could just "tell you where it hurts"? For those of us who have rabbits with more than one chronic ailment, a skilled communicator can be a key to rapid identification, and thus treatment, of the problem. Recently, Murray stopped eating less than five weeks after a molar trim when he had been going eight to ten weeks between trims. I asked his communicator to find out what was bothering him and he told her his teeth hurt. Sure enough, he had a nasty spur that had already lacerated his cheek. He was ready to eat by the time we got home from the vet!

Since animal communication is telepathic in nature, most communicators do not need to be physically with the animal to communicate. Some communicate with the animal via a phone conversation with the owner. Murray's primary communicator, who specializes in rabbits, requests a picture of your animal and the questions/issues via e-mail or her website (www.lagomorphs.com), conducts the session when your rabbit is receptive, and provides a written transcript of the session.

Most communicators agree that we are all born with the capacity to communicate with animals, but that for most of us the capability is "socialized" away at an early age. However, if you have a deep bond with your rabbit, you may periodically feel that you understand what he is trying to tell you—and you are probably right! Similarly, the deeper your connection is to your rabbit, the more likely it is that he will understand your efforts to communicate with him. This is why, throughout this book, I encourage you to take the time to explain to your rabbit what you are doing and why. This communication is important whether the subject is giving medicine, addressing a behavior problem, or explaining changes in his environment. Note, however, that even professional communicators often use another professional to communicate with their animals, especially about health-related issues. An owner's biases (either hopes or fears) can cloud the communication channels. Especially when the human-animal bond is deep, it may be easier for your rabbit to be completely honest when communicating through an uninvolved third party.

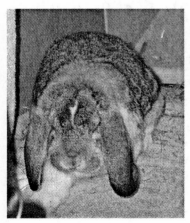

The newest member of our family is Thumper, a French Lop adopted from the shelter in October 2002 as a companion for my single female, Chip. HRH King Murray has let his communicator know several times that Thumper is not being properly "respectful" and "subservient." Because of his size (weighing in at just under 13 lbs.), Thumper has a definite "presence" in the household, and I am making special efforts to reassure Murray that he is, indeed, still King of the Household. (Photo by Kathy Smith)

KNOWING WHEN TO SAY GOODBYE

Some rabbits die suddenly, without warning. Some give up quickly after becoming ill. Some bravely hide their illness from you until it is too late. Others fight heroically to stay with you, against all odds. Whenever your rabbit dies, it will not be easy.

It is a sad fact of life that every living being is going to die sometime. When the time comes for a special rabbit friend, it is often difficult to make the decision to help them make the journey more easily. If you face this decision some day, take comfort in knowing that if your bunny is truly suffering, this is the last—and most important—gift you can give him. Be thankful that you can do this for your pet—it is a gift we cannot give our human loved ones.

If you feel you can handle it, ask to be with your rabbit during the procedure. Ask to spend a few minutes alone with your rabbit before the procedure. Pet him, tell him how much you love him and how much he will be missed. Reassure him his pain will soon be gone.

Ask your veterinarian to describe how the procedure will be done. Normally, drug is injected into a leg vein. You may want to request that your rabbit be given isoflourane gas first, to make the procedure easier on your bunny and on you. In very compromised rabbits, it is sometimes not possible for the doctor to find a vein. In these cases many do a "heart stick." If this is necessary, **insist** that your rabbit be **totally** anesthetized with isoflourane gas before the procedure is done. Most veterinarians will not let you be present during a heart stick—and you probably don't want to be. Instead, ask to hold your rabbit while he is gassed down, talk soothingly to him, and say goodbye while he is drifting off.

Choca Paws had to be euthanized barely a month after Smokey lost his battle with cancer. (Photo by Kathy Smith)

When Bunny Has Given Up

If your bunny is suffering from an acute, chronic, or terminal illness, it is often difficult to know whether he wants to continue to fight or is ready to give up. Here, it is important to remember that for critically ill rabbits some days will be better than others. Ups and downs are normal, and it is important to remember not to give up because of one or two bad days.

If you love your bunny, it is perfectly normal to wonder whether you are being selfish in keeping him alive or whether you are being selfish in considering euthanasia. Euthanasia should be considered only if your rabbit has a condition with no hope of recovery **and** he is either in pain that cannot be controlled by medication or has very poor quality of life. To help assess your rabbit's quality of life **from his perspective**, ask yourself the following questions:

• Does your rabbit still seem to enjoy your company and affection or the company and attention of a doting mate? If he is able, does he choose to be with you or his mate for comfort and companionship?

• Does your rabbit still enjoy food? Does he eagerly eat his favorite treats? If you are syringe-feeding, does he eat willingly?

• Does your rabbit still seem to find pleasure in some aspect of daily life, whether it is play, food, companionship, or simply stretching out comfortably in his favorite spot?

If the answer to any of the above questions is yes, your rabbit has not yet given up and you should not allow yourself to be talked into euthanasia by friends or family.

When a critically ill bunny exhibits one or more of the following behaviors, he is definitely having a "down" day:

• Refuses to eat even his favorite foods
• Fights syringe feeding or refuses to swallow
• Avoids all contact with you or his mate
• Sits for long periods with his back to you and his face in a corner

If this happens, don't be too quick to give up. Many critically ill rabbits will go through several short periods (two to three days) exhibiting one or more of the above behaviors, only to bounce back and have many good days before the next episode. During the down times, you may want to consult your veterinarian. She may be able to prescribe medication or suggest additional supportive measures to help your bunny feel better. Depending on your rabbit's personality, you may want to leave him alone or you may want to spend extra time holding him. Maintain a positive attitude, especially in your rabbit's presence; rabbits can sense your emotions, and the deeper your bond with your rabbit the more that is true. Make an extra effort to let your rabbit know how much you love him and encourage his fighting spirit.

When you see all of the above behaviors for an extended period of time (at least a week with no improvement) your bunny is telling you that he has given up. It is time to consider euthanasia.

When it is Time,
But Bunny is Not Ready

Some veterinarians feel that rabbits, in general, give up more easily than other species. However, a few special rabbits choose to fight serious illnesses, against all odds, and refuse to give up even when the battle is clearly lost. Frequently (though not always) these are rabbits who were neglected or abused during their early years; late in life they found a loving home and formed a deep bond with a human.

If you are the human in one of these relationships, it is especially hard to say goodbye to a rabbit who clearly is not ready to leave you. Sometimes, however, it is necessary to make that decision to prevent your rabbit from suffering a horrible death. When all medical options have been exhausted and your rabbit can no longer swallow something the consistency of canned pumpkin or his breathing becomes labored, it is time to say goodbye. No matter how much he wants to live, you cannot save him. What you can do is spare him—and yourself—the pain of death from suffocation or GI shutdown.

When we decided it was time for Smokey's final trip to the vet, he had been unable to eat anything except baby food for two days and his breathing had suddenly become labored. I had carried him to the living room to sit by the door in the sun one last time, and he had not moved from that position. Yet when I placed him in the shallow box, atop his best towels, for his final journey, he literally ran across the room and jumped onto his favorite shelf. He was clearly telling me he knew what was coming and he was not ready to leave me. I gently, but firmly, returned him to the box. I told him how much I loved him and how much I admired his courage, but that it was time to end his suffering. It was the hardest thing I've ever had to do. But in my heart I know it was the greatest gift I could give him. His death was peaceful, and I was grateful that I could be with him as he journeyed to a place where he could once again be whole.

Smokey a few days before losing his five month battle with cancer. (Photo by Kathy Smith)

COPING WITH LOSS

Whether your rabbit dies unexpectedly or following a long illness, you will face a number of practical and emotional challenges. The practical questions may include:

- How do I tell the rest of the family?
- Should I have a necropsy (an animal's autopsy) done?
- What do I want done with the body?
- Do I want another rabbit?

Emotional issues are often harder to address. If you were especially close to your rabbit, expect to go through the full grieving process—and realize that most people will not understand the depth of your grief. If you don't have friends who also have companion rabbits, you probably have a few friends who are true animal lovers. Spend as much time as you can with people who consider their dog or cat part of the family. These people will be able to empathize and give you comfort. Minimize contact with people whose attitude is "it was just a rabbit; get over it."

Resist the urge to blame yourself—or your veterinarian—for your rabbit's death. It won't bring your rabbit back and it is **not** what your rabbit would want! Hindsight is always 20/20—it is often easy to look back, with more information than you had at the time, and perhaps wish you had made a different decision. Remember that you and your veterinarian, working together, probably made the best decision you could with the information available at the time.

If you honestly believe that your rabbit's death was the result of a mistake you made, acknowledge your error, learn from it, and move on. In mental conversations with yourself, instead of saying, "What if…" or "If only…" say "Next time I will know to…." If you correspond with other rabbit owners (e.g., via e-mail), you may find it therapeutic to write about your experience. Not only will that help you work through your grief, sharing what you have learned could help countless other rabbits.

If you honestly believe that your rabbit's death was the result of veterinarian error, wait until you can be calm and rational, then sit down and discuss the problem with her. Don't accuse her of making a mistake. Instead, ask for her opinion on why your rabbit died and whether she would do anything differently next time. Listen objectively to her response, keeping in mind that medicine is not an exact science and your veterinarian is only human. Even if you feel your veterinarian made a poor choice, be open to the possibility that it **was** the best decision she could make with the information available to her.

At the end of your conversation you should either be comfortable that your veterinarian made the best decision possible or that she knows what she would do differently next time. If you don't feel this way, begin the search for a new veterinarian. Add to your list of questions something about how she would handle a situation like the one that led to your rabbit's death, but don't let that be the only question you focus on. After interviewing other veterinarians, you should either find someone new to work with or have renewed confidence in your present doctor.

When One of a Pair Dies

When one of a bonded pair dies, it is important for you, the human caretaker, to understand the impact on the survivor and to provide him with moral support. Remember that bunnies develop very deep bonds with their companions and will go through their own grieving process.

The most important thing you can do for the surviving member of a pair is to let him spend time with his mate's body. This allows him to accept that his companion is gone and will not be coming back. If you don't allow the survivor to see the body, he may continue to look everywhere for his mate and feel abandoned.

If your rabbit dies at home, his mate will probably be with him. If he dies at the vet's office, make every effort to arrange to bring the mate in to see the body or bring the body home for the mate to see. If you take a critically ill rabbit to be euthanized, take his companion along. He will provide comfort on the trip and will be there to see the body afterwards.

Unless your rabbit was euthanized in the final stages of a critical illness, it is wise to do a necropsy (an animal's autopsy), especially if the dead rabbit was part of a bonded group. The necropsy often involves taking tissue samples for a pathologist to examine microscopically for a better explanation of the cause of disease/death. If your rabbit died of a contagious disease or an environmental hazard (such as poisoning), your surviving rabbits may also be in danger. The sooner you pinpoint the cause of death, the sooner you can begin treating or protecting the survivors. And, if the cause of death was **not** something that affects your surviving rabbits, you can begin to relax and work through the grieving process with them.

After losing a mate, the survivor will go through a grieving period and will need extra TLC from you. Spend as much time with him as possible. Physical contact is especially important at this time. If his appetite seems off, tempt him with his favorite foods. Sit on the floor and eat with him—remember that eating is a social activity for rabbits. Monitor his food intake, fecal output, and activity level carefully and consult your veterinarian if he stops eating completely or if fecals become very small. Some rabbits will find comfort if you give them a stuffed animal the same size and color as their deceased companion.

Most rabbits who lose a mate will ultimately be happier with a new companion. Observe your rabbit closely and listen to your heart. When you feel the time is right, contact the nearest rescue group or shelter and arrange to take your rabbit to pick out a new companion. It is always best to introduce rabbits to each other in neutral territory (a place where neither bunny has been before) to minimize territorial behavior. And no matter how well an initial meeting goes, bonding needs to be a slow and cautious process. An excellent article on bonding is available at http://www.rabbitnetwork.org/articles/bond.shtml.

When Frankie died, Goldie and Murray comforted each other. When Goldie died a mere five months later, Murray made it clear he did not want another companion and began his "reign" as King of the house. (Photo by Kathy Smith)

The Importance of Necropsies

Ideally, you and your veterinarian should discuss attitudes toward necropsies (the veterinary equivalent of an autopsy) in the early stages of your relationship—preferably before your bunny becomes sick. In their grief, many people have trouble agreeing to a necropsy. However, unless your rabbit was euthanized in the final stages of a critical illness, a necropsy is important for a number of reasons.

If you have other rabbits in your household, a necropsy with histopathology (tissue samples sent in to a pathologist) is important to rule out the presence of contagious disease or environmental toxins that may shorten the lives of your other rabbits. The sooner you identify a problem, if it is present, the better chance you will have of saving your other rabbits. And if the necropsy uncovers nothing that is a threat to your surviving rabbits, you can relax knowing that the question was asked and answered.

Necropsy results can help caretakers move beyond feelings of guilt we may have about a rabbit's death. In our grief, we often obsess about what we might have done differently. Did we miss a subtle sign that something was wrong? Was the problem one that could have been treated if we (or our veterinarian) had done something sooner? In most cases a necropsy will confirm that there was nothing we could have done to prevent our beloved companion's death. If we (or our veterinarian) **did** miss something, however subtle, the information from the necropsy gives us a chance to learn from our mistake and hopefully not repeat it.

Stormy was a cuddle bunny who loved nothing more than to be cradled in my arms like a baby. George could snap his fingers at Stormy's gate and he would always come running to be petted. He would tug at my pant leg while I was brushing my teeth and when I delivered his salad, he was always more interested in attention than food. When Stormy died of pneumonia just before Christmas, George and I were devastated. His necropsy results helped me accept that there was nothing we could have done to save him. (Photo by Kathy Smith)

Final Arrangements

It is not a pleasant thing to think about, but now is the time to consider what you want done with your rabbit's remains. This is a personal decision that must be made by each caretaker family. Religious beliefs and attitudes toward death will influence your decision. Make the choice that is right for you and your family—don't allow outsiders to dictate your choice.

If this is not your first pet—or if you already know how you would want things handled—discuss your preferences with your veterinarian's office now. Most veterinarian offices will be willing to keep your instructions in your file and simply confirm their execution when the time comes. This will minimize the decisions you need to make and the questions you must answer when you are grieving.

Many people find comfort in burying their pets in their back yard. Before choosing this option, consider whether you plan to be in your current home long-term and how you will feel about your decision if you decide to move in the future. Also, some cities may have ordinances prohibiting burying pets in the yard, so check with your city before settling on this option.

Many cities have pet crematoriums that offer you the choice of individual or mass cremation. If cremation appeals to you, ask your veterinarian's office about the availability and price of cremation. Find out if the crematorium does pick-up and delivery (sometimes at an extra charge), or if you will have to get the body to them. If you don't want the ashes returned to you, mass cremation is an economical option. Individual cremations are significantly more expensive, but allow the ashes to be returned to you. Some people find comfort in scattering the ashes in a meaningful setting. Others choose to keep the ashes and purchase an attractive urn for them. Again, the choice should be what feels right for you and your family.

Many pet crematoriums also have a cemetery where you can choose to have your pet buried. They offer a variety of services including personalized headstones and memorial services. Again, your veterinarian's office should be aware of the choices available in your city.

Whether you choose burial or cremation, you may find comfort in holding some kind of memorial service for your rabbit. This can be a formal ceremony through a pet cemetery, an informal family ceremony, or a solitary moment of personal meditation. A memorial ceremony is an excellent way to help children pay tribute to a special animal.

Some people want to do something tangible in memory of a beloved pet. They may choose to plant a tree, volunteer at or adopt from a local shelter, or make a donation to a veterinary school or rescue organization in memory of their pet.

Smokey relaxes on his bunny pillow just two months before being diagnosed with cancer. The original <u>Rabbit Health 101</u> was written as a tribute to his courage. (Photo by Kathy Smith)

Deciding to Welcome Another Rabbit Into Your Heart

After losing a special animal companion, most people struggle with the question of when—and if—they should welcome another pet into their home and heart. There is no right answer. This is a personal decision that must be made by each family, taking into account the feelings of each family member, human and animal.

Some people swear they will never have another pet because the pain of loss is too great. Others immediately get another animal because they can't stand the sense of emptiness. Most take some time to grieve, and in time decide to welcome another animal into their lives. Animals add so much to our lives—try to at least remain open to the possibility of another animal some day.

Whatever you decide, it should be your family's decision. Don't allow well-meaning family or friends to make the decision for you. Make it clear that you do **not** want them to bring you a new rabbit—or any other animal—to replace the one you lost. If your rabbit left a mate, he will help you decide when it is time for another rabbit and it is best if you let him pick out his new companion. It is always best to introduce rabbits to each other in neutral territory (a place where neither bunny has been before) to minimize territorial behavior. And no matter how well an initial meeting goes, bonding needs to be a slow and cautious process.

When you are ready to start thinking about another rabbit, keep in mind that you are not trying to replace the one you lost. Instead, view it as a decision to share the love you had for him with another rabbit. In time, most of us realize that this is what our beloved companion would have wanted. Often, especially if you have had an truly deep bond with your rabbit, your next rabbit will come along at what seems like exactly the right time—almost as if your special companion arranged it.

Some people are drawn to another rabbit who looks like the one they recently lost. This is fine as long as you recognize that animals, like people, each have their own individual personality. There will never be another rabbit like the one you lost—and it is unfair to a new rabbit to expect that. Don't adopt another rabbit—or any other animal—until you are ready to accept him on his own terms.

If you have always had an "only" bunny, consider adopting a bonded pair or trio. Rabbits enjoy the companionship of other rabbits, and it is great fun to watch them interact with each other. In each member of the group you may see traits that remind you of your former rabbit—but with a group you will be less likely to expect one of them to be exactly like him.

Finally, when you are ready for another rabbit, please contact your nearest Humane Society, shelter, or other rescue organization. There is nothing as rewarding as adopting an animal who has been neglected, abused, or abandoned and watching him blossom in the light of your love.

I am convinced that after Smokey died his spirit guided me to adopt The Trio, Murray, Goldie, and Frankie. (Photo by Kathy Smith)

HELPFUL HINTS

If you have never performed the procedures discussed in this section, be sure to have your veterinarian **show** you how to perform them correctly. Don't be surprised if something that looked simple at the vet's office seems impossible the first time you have to do it by yourself. Remember, at the vet's office you had an extra pair of hands—and those belonged to a highly skilled professional! Everyone struggles the first few times. The purpose of this section is to share ideas and techniques that have worked for people I know. Remember, every bunny is an individual and what works for one bunny may fail miserably for another.

General Hints

Whether you're taking a temperature, examining your bunny, or giving fluids or medications, it always helps to do the following:

1.   Make sure you have everything you need in one place and as ready as possible **before** you pick up your bunny. It is much easier to fill a syringe, lubricate a thermometer, or change the needle on a bag of fluids while you have both hands available.

2.   Approach your bunny in a calm, confident manner, establish eye contact, and explain to your bunny what you need to do and why. Talking to your rabbit has a calming effect and shows respect.

3.   Find a position that is comfortable for both you and your bunny. Some people prefer to perform exams and give medications sitting on the floor. The advantage is that if your bunny does bolt, he is less likely to hurt himself. On the other hand he may be more likely to try to escape because he is on his turf. Others find it easier to work standing up with their bunny on a surface such as a washer/dryer, kitchen or bathroom counter, or baby's changing table.

Giving Oral Medications and Syringe Feeding

At some point you will probably have to give your bunny some type of oral medication. Some medications are available as a liquid while others are available only as tablets or capsules. If your rabbit's medication is a pill, some veterinarians will pre-mix it for you with sterile water while others will give you pills along with instructions on how to mix each dose. In general, liquids are more convenient for you (since you don't have to mix each dose) but pills have a much longer shelf-life.

Most liquid medicines should be shaken before being measured to ensure even distribution of the active ingredients. If the liquid has a dropper and your veterinarian gives you a dose in droppers (or drops), it is a good idea to also ask for the precise dose in cc or ml. While it is sometimes convenient to use a dropper, you also run a greater risk of spilling the medication (because the dropper is also the lid). This is especially true if the dose is 1½ droppers and you have to get that ½ dropper from a nearly-empty bottle while holding a rabbit who doesn't want more medicine!

Pills can sometimes be given to a rabbit by hiding them in a favorite treat such as a raisin or a small piece of banana. If you give medicine in a treat, watch carefully to make sure your rabbit doesn't eat the treat and leave the pill.

The most common way to give a pill to a rabbit is to crush and dissolve it in a small amount of water (usually 1–2cc) and administer it with a syringe. Some people prefer to give oral medications with their bunny sitting on a flat surface while others prefer to hold their rabbit (in an upright position). You'll need to find what works best for you—and it may change depending on the bunny you are medicating. If your rabbit fights his medicine, try adding a few drops of grenadine (not more than a 50/50 ratio of grenadine to water) or try mixing with juice instead of water.

Any time you give your rabbit food or medicine with a syringe, remember the following safety tips:

- **Always** hold your rabbit in a position so he is able to swallow easily

- **Always** point the syringe toward the side of your rabbit's mouth and empty it slowly, making sure he swallows what is in his mouth before adding more

- **Never** point the syringe straight toward your rabbit's throat—this is a good way to choke him and/or get liquid in his lungs.

Giving Sub-Q Fluids and Injections

If you have several bunnies or a chronically ill bunny, chances are good that you will need to learn to give sub-q fluids and/or injections. If you are squeamish about needles (as I was), take comfort in knowing that most bunnies tolerate these procedures quite well.

When giving fluids, you will need to find a place that is comfortable for you and your bunny **and** has somewhere you can hang the fluids far enough above the bunny that the drip works. You also may want to be near a sink or drain just in case your bunny dislodges the needle—or in case you accidentally stick the needle through two layers of skin. I use the top of the washer and hang the fluid bag from the cabinet above it. Others use a bathroom counter and hang the bag from the mirror over the sink. Unless your rabbit is running a fever, your vet may have you warm the fluids by running the line through a bowl of very warm water or by wrapping the bag in a heading pad. **Do not** warm fluids in a microwave since microwaves do not get heat evenly distributed.

To give fluids, tent the skin and **confidently** insert the needle—inserting slowly is more painful and more likely to cause trauma to the injection site. Make sure the needle is all the way in (to avoid getting fluid between the layers of skin) but does not go through both layers of skin. Once the needle is in, release the tented skin, gently move the needle to ensure it isn't obstructed, and start the drip. If fluids are flowing more slowly than normal, check for a "flat" spot where the IV line was shut off (squeeze it back to round) and make sure there are no kinks in the line. You may also need to move the needle slightly to encourage proper flow.

Many rabbits will actually groom themselves or nibble on food while you give fluids. If your rabbit is restless, try lifting him in his litter-box to the appropriate surface. The sides of the litter-box will make it more difficult for him to squirm away and if you have hay in the litter-box he may decide to nibble on it.

When giving injections, it is important to get the needle completely through the skin. Failure to do this can create sore spots (sterile abscesses) on your rabbit's back. If you are giving both sub-q fluids and an injection, check with your veterinarian to see if it is OK to inject the medication into the fluid pocket immediately after giving fluids. With many injections, this helps reduce the sting of the shot.

RESOURCES

Books (General Care)

Hop to It: A Guide to Training Your Pet Rabbit by Samantha Fraser
House Rabbit Handbook, Third Edition by Marinell Harriman
The Essential Rabbit by Betsy Sikora Siino
Why Does My Rabbit? by Anne McBride

Books (Veterinary)

Ferrets, Rabbits, and Rodents Clinical Medicine, Hillyer and Quesenberry, eds.
Rodent and Rabbit Medicine, Laber-Laird, Swindle and Flecknell eds.
Textbook of Rabbit Medicine by Frances Harcourt-Brown

Books (Alternative Medicine)

Flower Essences: Flower Essences for Animals by Lila Devi
                   Bach Flower Remedies for Animals by Helen Graham and
                   Gregory Vlamis
T-Touch: The Tellington Ttouch by Linda Tellington-Jones
Communication: Straight From the Horse's Mouth by Amelia Kinkade
Aromatherapy: Holistic Aromatherapy for Animal by Kristen Leigh Bell
Massage: The Relaxed Rabbit: Massage for your Pet Bunny by
                   Chandra Beal (coming soon!)
General: Animal Healing and Vibrational Medicine by Sage
                   Holloway
                   The Holistic Animal Handbook by Kate Solisti-Matelon

Online

House Rabbit Network: http://www.rabbitnetwork.org
Rabbit References: http://www.morfz.com/rabrefs.html
Flower Essence: http://www.anaflora.com,
http://www.animalsinourhearts.com/ commune/flower1.htm
T-touch: http://tteam-ttouch.com/

Animal Communication: http://www.animalsinourhearts.com/, http://www.animaltalk.net/

E-mail Lists: YahooGroups offers numerous Rabbit e-mail groups with a variety of focuses. Two groups that focus primarily on health and/or behavior are: HOUSEBUN, a low volume, moderated list, restricted to topics of health, care and behavior as they relate to **house** rabbits. ETHERBUN, a low-to-moderate volume, unmoderated list with topics **strictly** restricted to topics of rabbit health and behavior.

Specialty Lab Testing Facilities

As of March 1, 2000, both Pasteurella and *E. cuniculi* testing (previously done at the University of Missouri Research Animal Diagnostic and Investigative Laboratory [RADIL]) are being performed by:

Sound Diagnostics (Dr. Barbara Deeb)   206-363-0787 (voice)
1222 NE 145th Street   206-383-0948 (fax)
Seattle, WA 98155-7134

Thyroid serum testing for rabbits is done by a central laboratory in British Columbia. The following address is used for submitting samples from the U.S.—have your veterinarian call for details:

C.L.   800-663-1425 (voice)
PMB 80
250 H St.
Blaine, WA 98230

Consulting Veterinarians (Vet-to-Vet Consultations)

If your veterinarian needs to consult on a difficult case, she may have her own network of colleagues to call on. If not—or if her network fails to yield the information she is looking for—the following are **some** of the experienced rabbit veterinarians who are available for consultations **with their colleagues.** Keep in mind that whether your veterinarian is looking for someone who has dealt with a rare disorder or is seeking new approaches to a common problem, it may take several calls to locate the information. And while many veterinarians consult with colleagues at no charge, some veterinarians—including some listed here—do charge a consultation fee. In addition to paying any fees charged by the other vet, remember to offer to pay **your** vet for the time she spends consulting for you as well as any long-distance charges.

Teresa Bradley, DVM	816-331-3120	(MO)	belancl@aol.com
Thomas Chlebecek, DVM	808-262-9621	(HI)	
Bronwyn Dawson, DVM	626-303-7881	(CA)	
Kenneth Dazen, DVM or David Kupersmith, DVM	856-751-2122	(NJ)	
Barbara Deeb, DVM	206-365-1102	(WA)	
Carolynn Harvey, DVM	510-654-8375	(CA)	ch2@aol.com
Jeffrey Jenkins, DVM	800-379-6842	(CA)	drexotic@aol.com
Sari Kanfer, DVM	626-303-7881	(CA)	
Susan Kelleher, DVM	954-968-7171	(FL)	AuntNoon@cofs.net
Diane Mitchell, DVM	425-483-5834	(WA)	
Nancy Modglin, DVM (Acupuncture)	909-796-4277	(CA)	
Scott Sloan, DVM (Orthopedic Surgeon)	626-798-5901	(CA)	
Scott J. Stahl, DVM, DABVP-Avian			sstahldvm@aol.com

Other Resources for Veterinary Professionals Only

Antech Laboratories Consulting Services	888-VET-INFO
IDEXX Laboratory Consulting Service	800-444-4210
Exotic DVM Listserv	ExoticDVM@yahoogroups.com
Veterinary Information Network	http://vin.com

Non-Profit Bunny-Friendly Suppliers (All Proceeds Help Rescued Animals. All groups have adoptable rabbits and are great resources for rabbit care information.)

Best Little Rabbit, Rodent & Ferret House
14325 Lake City Way NE
Seattle WA 98125

Hay, food, and toys for your rabbit.
http://www.Rabbitrodentferret.org
206-365-9105 (voice)

Bunny Bunch Boutique
P. O. Box 2583
Chino, CA 91708

Quality food, hay, toys. Fun stuff for humans!
http://www.bunnybunchboutique.com
866-88BUNNY or 909-591-7200

Rabbit Rescue Shop
P.O. Box 40460
Downey, CA 90240

Great rabbit toys. Rabbit-themed items for humans
http://www.rabbitshop.com
562-862-8844

Zooh Corner Rabbit Rescue
P.O. Box 836
Claremont, CA 91711

Hay, food, and great rabbit toys.
www.mybunny.org
909-868-BUNI

For Profit Bunny-Friendly Suppliers

American Pet Diner (hay and pellets)
HC 62, Box 186
Eureka, NV 89316

http://www.americanpetdiner.com
800-656-2691 (voice)
775-237-5118 (fax)

Bunny Bytes (hay, pellets, litter, and toys)
P.O. Box 1581
Kent, WA 98075

http://www.bunnybytes.com
888-563-9300 (voice)

The Busy Bunny (edible toys, treats, and hay)
P.O. Box 1023
San Bruno, CA 94066-7023

http://www.busybunny.com
650-872-2920 (best times: M–F after 3:00 pm
or Sat. & Sun. 10:00 a.m. to 10:00 p.m. PST)

Cats & Rabbits & More (Promotes adoptions)
P.O. Box 2754
Spring Valley, CA 91979

Great gifts for and about rabbits.
Check out the Cottontail Cottage.
http://www.catsandrabbitsandmore.com

KW Cages (exercise pens)
9565 Pathway St.
Santee, CA 92071

http://www.kwcages.com
800-447-CAGE (voice)
619-596-4008 (fax)

Leith Petwerks (hay, pellets, toys, cages)
1276 Old Capital Pike
Bloomington, IN 47403

http://leithpetwerks.com
812-824-1488 (voice)
978-246-1299 (fax)

Oxbow Hay Company (hay and pellets)
29012 Mill Road
Murdock, NE 68407

http://www.oxbowhay.com
800-249-0366 (voice)

RabbitsNmore (Promotes shelter adoptions)
186 Country Club Gate Center
Pacific Grove, CA 93950

Hay, food, toys, plus unique gifts for humans
http://www.rabbitsnmore.com
831-657-0507

Special Needs Supplies

Doggon' Wheels
P.O. Box 1503
Livingston, MT 59047

http://www.doggon.com
888-736-4466

K-9 Cart Co.
656 SE Bayshore Drive, Suite #2
Oak Harbor, WA 98277

http://www.k9carts.com
800-578-6960 (voice)
360-675-1809 (Fax)

FURTHER READING

For more information on some of the topics covered in this book, you may wish to read the following articles or visit the websites listed below. Articles and websites listed here are grouped by subject and subjects are listed in the order they appear in this book. Within each subject, websites are listed first, followed by articles listed beginning with those most recently written. Because medicine is a constantly evolving science, the information in any article may be superceded by more recent information. As always, consult your veterinarian for the latest information on any medical subject.

Neuters and Spays

About Rabbit Spaying and Neutering. Jeffrey R. Jenkins, DVM. San Diego Rabbit News, Winter 1998.

To Neuter or Not to Neuter, That is the Question. Susan Brown, DVM. Chicago House Rabbit News, Volume 4 # 2, Spring, 1997.

Gastrointestinal System

Ileus in Domestic Rabbits. Dana Krempels, Mary Cotter and Gil Stanzione. Exotic DVM, Volume 2.4. http://fig.cox.miami.edu/Faculty/Dana/ileus.pdf

GastroIntestinal Stasis, The Silent Killer. Dana M. Krempels, Ph.D. Copyright 1997. Revised: May 1999. http://fig.cox.miami.edu/Faculty/Dana/ileus.html

GI Disorders in the House Rabbit. Anne Gentry, DVM. Harelines (Ohio House Rabbit Society), Volume 2 # 1, Winter, 1998.

A Typical Case of Enteritis and Enterotoxemia—Or What You Can Expect to See. Sandi Ackerman. Washington House Rabbit News, Volume 4 # 2, December 1994.

A Typical Hair Blockage Scenario—Or What You Can Expect to See. Sandi Ackerman. Washington House Rabbit News, Volume 4 # 2, December 1994.

Rabbit GI Physiology and Diet. Susan Brown, DVM. Rabbit Health News, # 11, April 1994.

Infections

Myxomatosis. Michael J. Murray, DVM. www.kindplanet.org/myxo.html (written for caretakers)

Myxomatosis in Rabbits. Michael J. Murray, DVM. www.kindplanet.org/myxo2.html (written for veterinarians)

VHD: www.kindplanet.org/vhd

Tearing and Runny Eyes. Jeffrey R. Jenkins, DVM. San Diego Rabbit News, Fall, 1997.

Pasteurella: What Is It and Should You Fear It? Jeffrey R. Jenkins, DVM. San Diego Rabbit News, Spring, 1995.

Fleas

New Products Make Flea Control Easy. Jeffrey R. Jenkins, DVM. San Diego Rabbit News, Summer, 1998.

A Discussion of Flea Control. Susan Brown, DVM. Chicago House Rabbit News, Volume 4 # 3, Summer, 1997.

Dental Disease

Dental Problems in Rabbits. Sari Kanfer. Zooh Corner Rabbit Rescue (www.mybunny.org).

Dental Disease in Rabbits. Cathy Palomar, DVM. Harelines (Ohio House Rabbit Society), Volume 3 # 2, Spring/Summer 1999.

Does My Rabbit Need a Tooth Trim? Natalie Antinoff, DVM, Diplomate ABVP (Avian). The Rabbit Review (Bunny Buddies, Houston, TX). June 1999.

What You Should Know about Your Rabbit's Teeth. Janet Bigger, DVM. The Bunny Thymes, Volume 3 # 12, December 1997/January 1998.

Oral Health In Rabbits. Carolynn Harvey, DVM. House Rabbit Journal, Volume 3 # 9, Fall/Winter, 1996-1997.

Causes and Treatment of Common Dental Problems in Rabbits. Jeffrey R. Jenkins, DVM. San Diego Rabbit News, Summer, 1995.

Coccidia

Coccidia in the Intestines, Liver. Jeffrey R. Jenkins, DVM. <u>San Diego Rabbit News</u>, Fall 1995.

Red Urine

Red Urine: Blood or Plant Pigment. Sandi Ackerman in consultation with Barbara Deeb, DVM, MS. <u>House Rabbit Journal</u>, Volume 3 # 1, Winter, 1994.

E. cuniculi

Prevention and Treatment of Encephalitozoon cuniculi Infection in Rabbits with Fenbendazole. Suter C, Mullin-Doblies UU, Hatt JM, Deplazes P. Veterinary Record April 14, 2001.

Update on Testing and Treatment of Rabbits with E-Cuniculi. Jeffrey R. Jenkins, DVM. <u>San Diego Rabbit News</u>, Spring, 1997.

E-cuniculi: Cause of Unexplained Neurological Diseases. Jeffrey R. Jenkins, DVM. <u>San Diego Rabbit News</u>, Winter 1997.

Head Tilt

Head Tilt: Causes and Treatment. Sandi Ackerman in consultation with Barbara Deeb, DVM, MS. <u>House Rabbit Journal</u>, Volume 3 # 8, Summer, 1996.

Bladder Sludge/Kidney Disease

Preventing Kidney and Bladder Stones in Rabbits. Anne Downes, DVM. <u>The Bunny Thymes</u>, Volume 4 # 18, April/May 1999.

Bladder "Sludge" and Stones. Natalie Antinoff, DVM, Diplomate ABVP (Avian). <u>The Rabbit Review</u> (Bunny Buddies, Houston, Texas). October 1998.

Bladder Stones and Sludge: Cystic Calculi in Rabbit. Susan Brown, DVM. <u>Chicago House Rabbit News</u>, Volume 5 # 3, Fall, 1998.

Bladder Stones and Sludge. Susan Brown, DVM. <u>Chicago House Rabbit News</u>, Volume 5 # 2, Summer, 1998.

Diapering a Rabbit. Susan Smith, PhD. <u>Wisconsin House Rabbit News,</u> Volume 5 # 1, Spring, 1998.

What You Should Know About Kidney Disease. Anne Downes, DVM. <u>The Bunny Thymes</u>, Volume 3 # 12, Febraury/March 1998.

Lowering Blood Calcium. Compiled by Kathleen Wilsbasch, Phd. <u>House Rabbit Journal</u>, Volume 3 # 5, Summer, 1995.

Abscesses

New Treatment for Jaw Abscesses. Jeffrey R. Jenkins, DVM. <u>San Diego Rabbit News</u>, Winter, 1999.

Abscesses in Rabbits. Anne Downes, DVM. <u>The Bunny Thymes</u>, Volume 4 # 14, June/July 1997.

Arthritis

Old Bunny Paralysis. Susan Brown, DVM. <u>Chicago House Rabbit News</u>, Volume 2 # 3, Spring, 1996; Volume 2 # 4, Summer, 1996; Volume 3 # 1, Fall, 1996; Volume 3 # 2, Winter, 1997.

Antibiotics

Bicillin Protocol: http://moorelab.sbs.umass.edu/~mrosenfield/bicillin/

Antibiotic-Induced Enteritis and Enterotoxemia. Jeffrey R. Jenkins, DVM. <u>San Diego Rabbit News</u>, Summer 1997.

Chloramphenicol in Veterinary Medicine. J. F. R. Hird, DVM and A. Knifton, DVM. <u>The Veterinary Record</u>, September 1996.

Analgesia

The Importance of Analgesia for Pet Rabbits. Susan Brown, DVM <u>Chicago Rabbit News</u>, Volume 6 #3, Holiday 1999 and Volume 7 # 1, Spring 2000.

What is Pain? Why and How Is It Treated in Rabbits? Joanne Paul Murphy, DVM, Diplomate ACZM. <u>House Rabbit Journal</u>, Volume 3 # 10, Spring/Summer 1997.

Anesthesia

Anesthesia in Rabbits. Natalie Antinoff, DVM, Diplomate ABVP (Avian). <u>The Rabbit Review</u> (Bunny Buddies, Houston, Texas). February 1999.

Taking the Fear out of Rabbit Anesthesia. Susan Brown, DVM. <u>Chicago House Rabbit News</u>, Volume 5 # 4, Holiday 1998; Volume 6 # 1, Spring, 1999.

Alternative Medicine

http://www.altvetmed.com

Harry Goes to the Chiropractor. Kathy Nolan. House Rabbit Journal, Volume 3 # 12, Winter/Spring, 1998.

Evaluating Harry. Marc L. Sommer, DVM. House Rabbit Journal, Volume 3 # 12, Winter/Spring, 1998.

Miscellaneous

Care of the Elderly Rabbit. Jeffrey R. Jenkins, DVM. San Diego Rabbit News, Spring, 1999.

Caring for the Geriatric Bunny. Susan Smith, PhD. Wisconsin House Rabbit News, Volume 5 # 1, Spring, 1998.

To De(claw) or Not to De(claw)—That is the Question. Joanne Paul-Murphy, DVM. Washington House Rabbit News, Volume 5 # 2,3,4, October 1996.

Printed in the United States
23420LVS00004B/150

9 780595 281374